flowers

THE PHOTO BOOK

FOR THE
GARDEN
LOVERS

"A flower cannot blossom witho
ut sunshine, and man cannot
live without love."

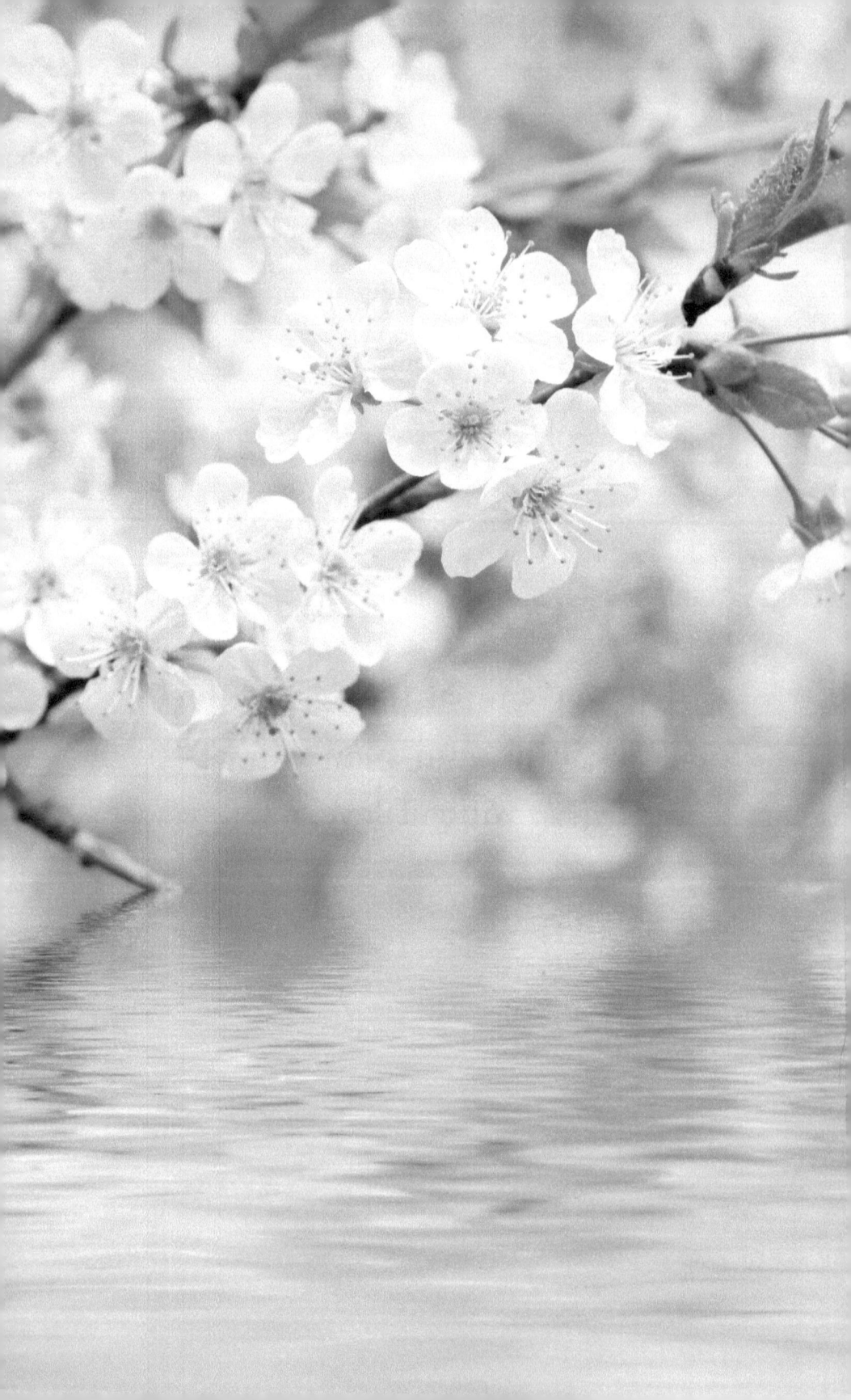

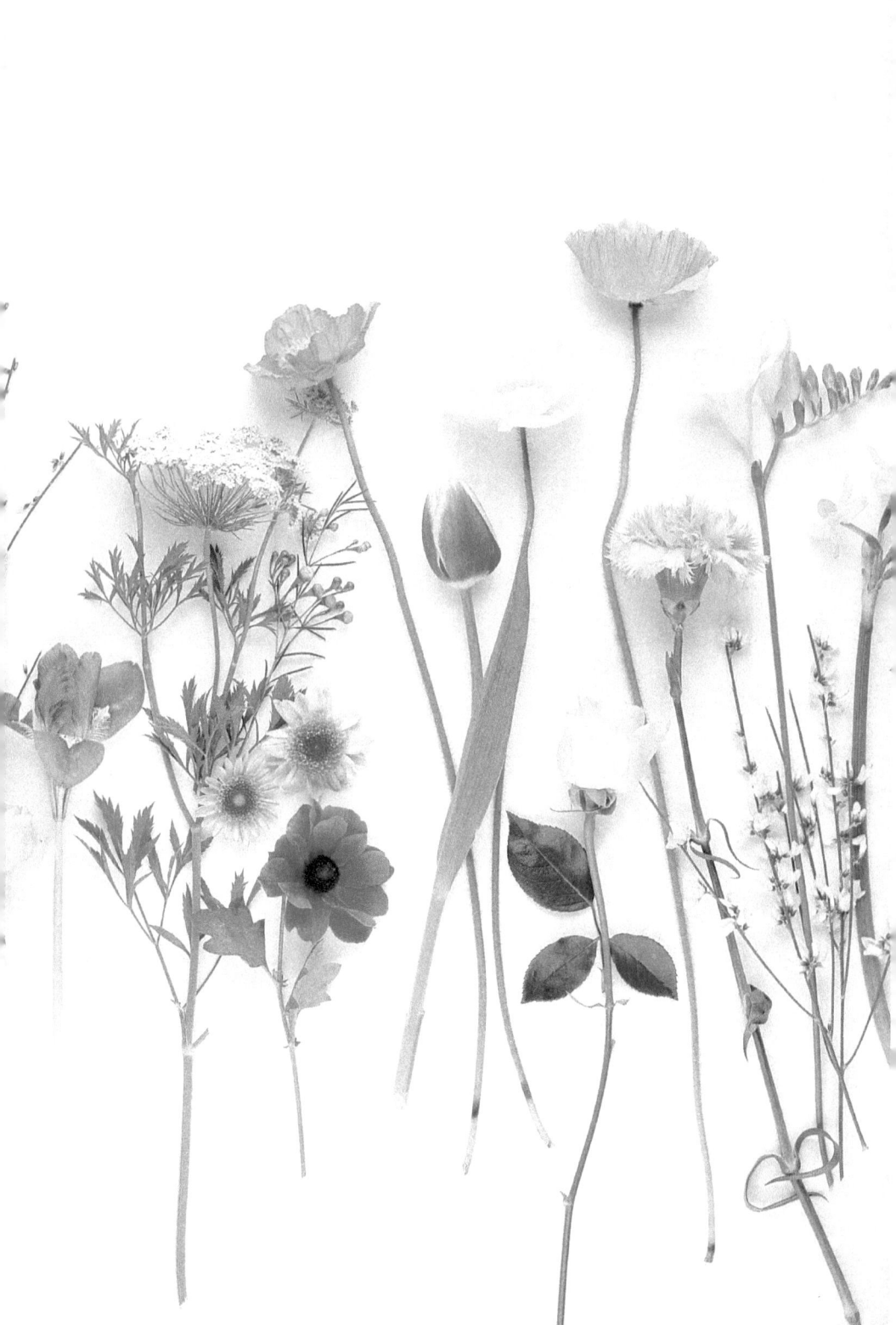

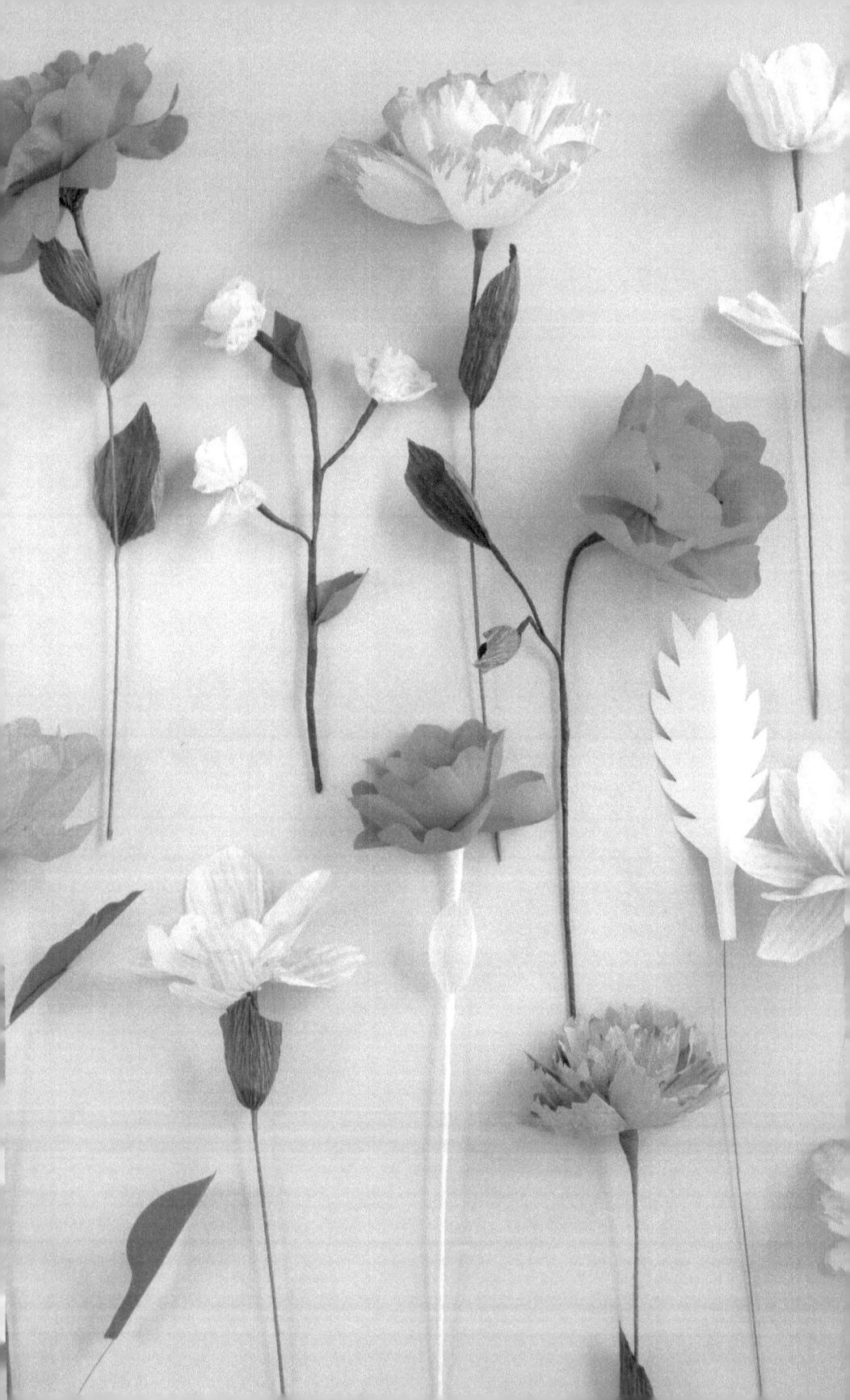

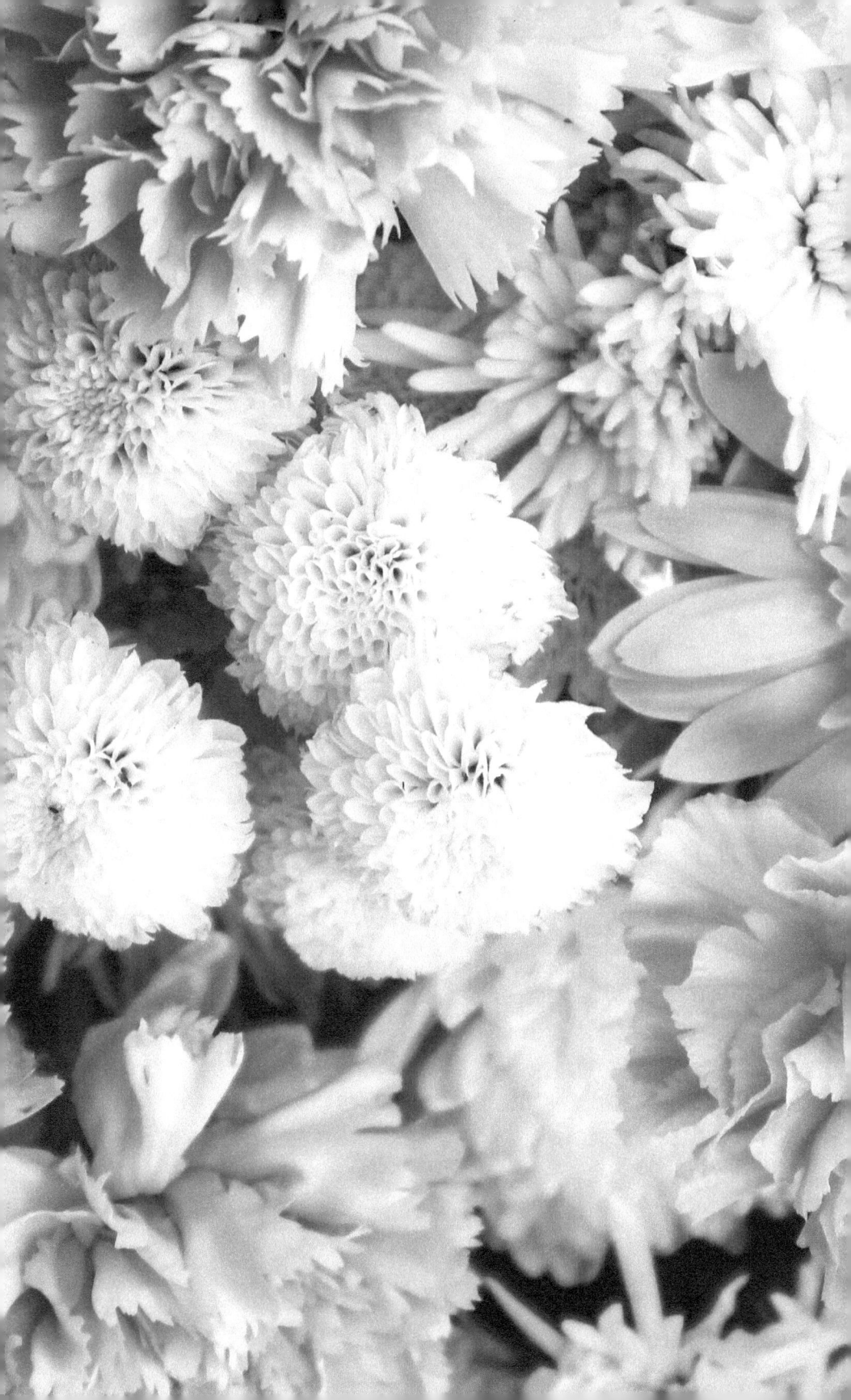

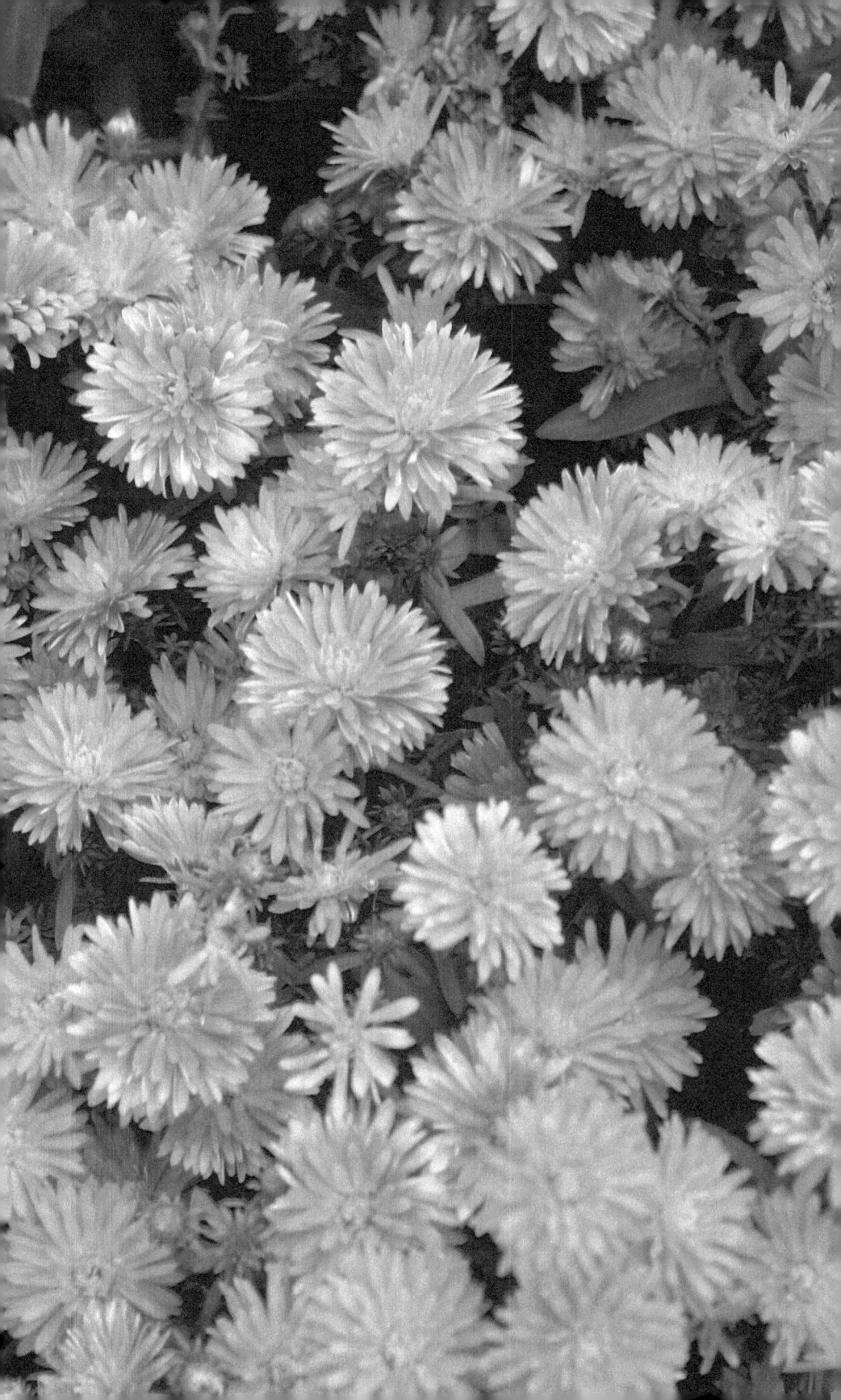

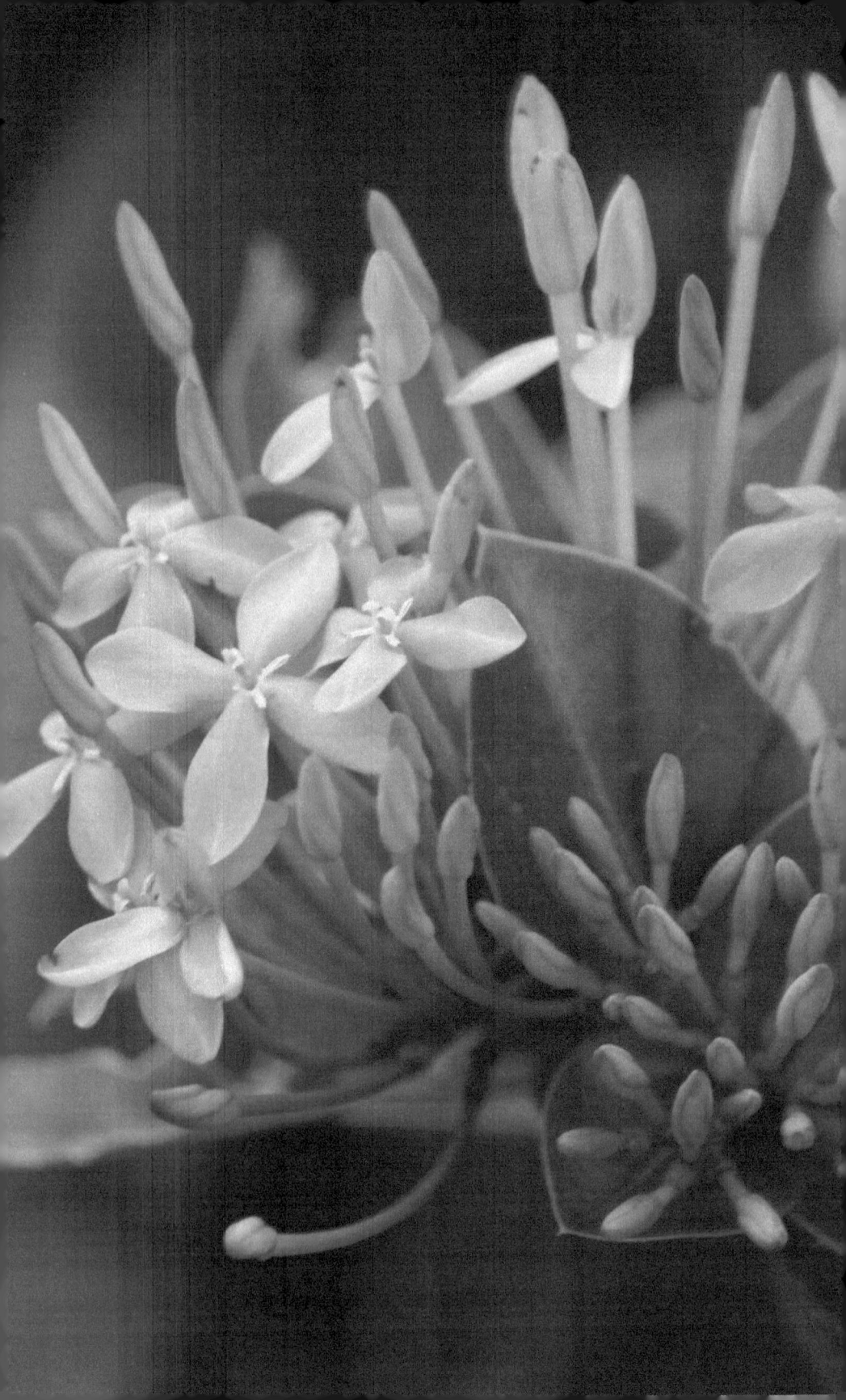

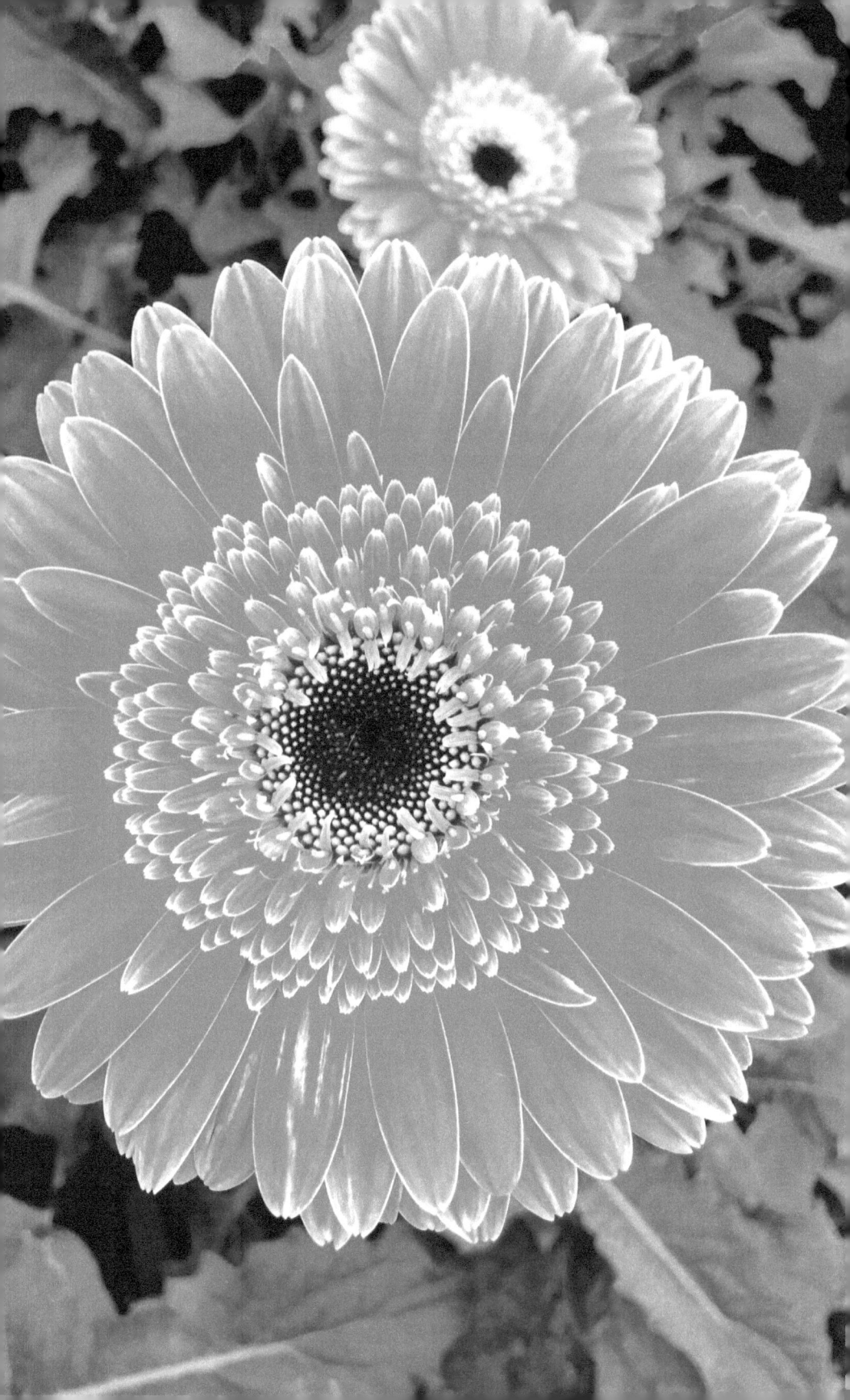

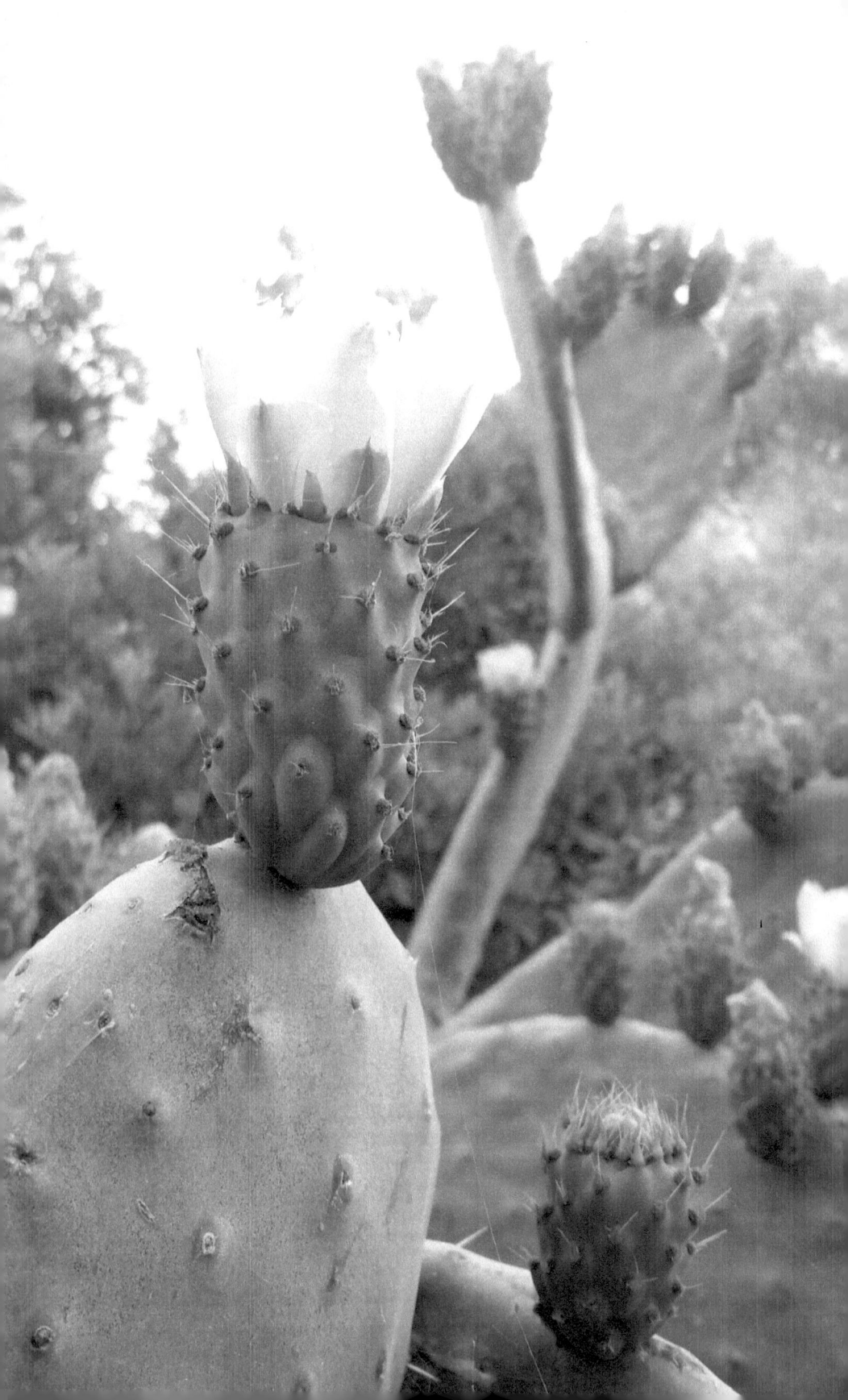

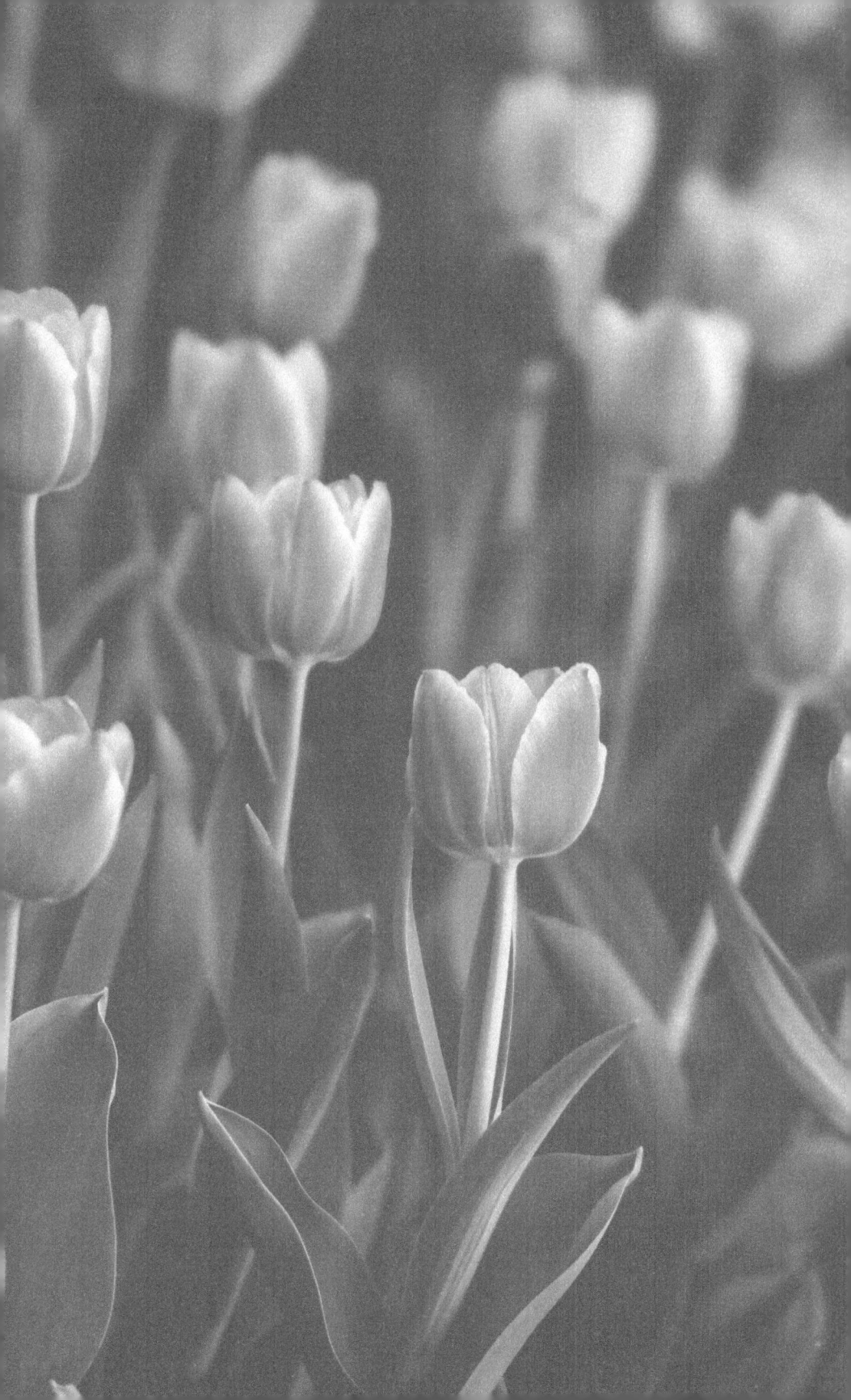

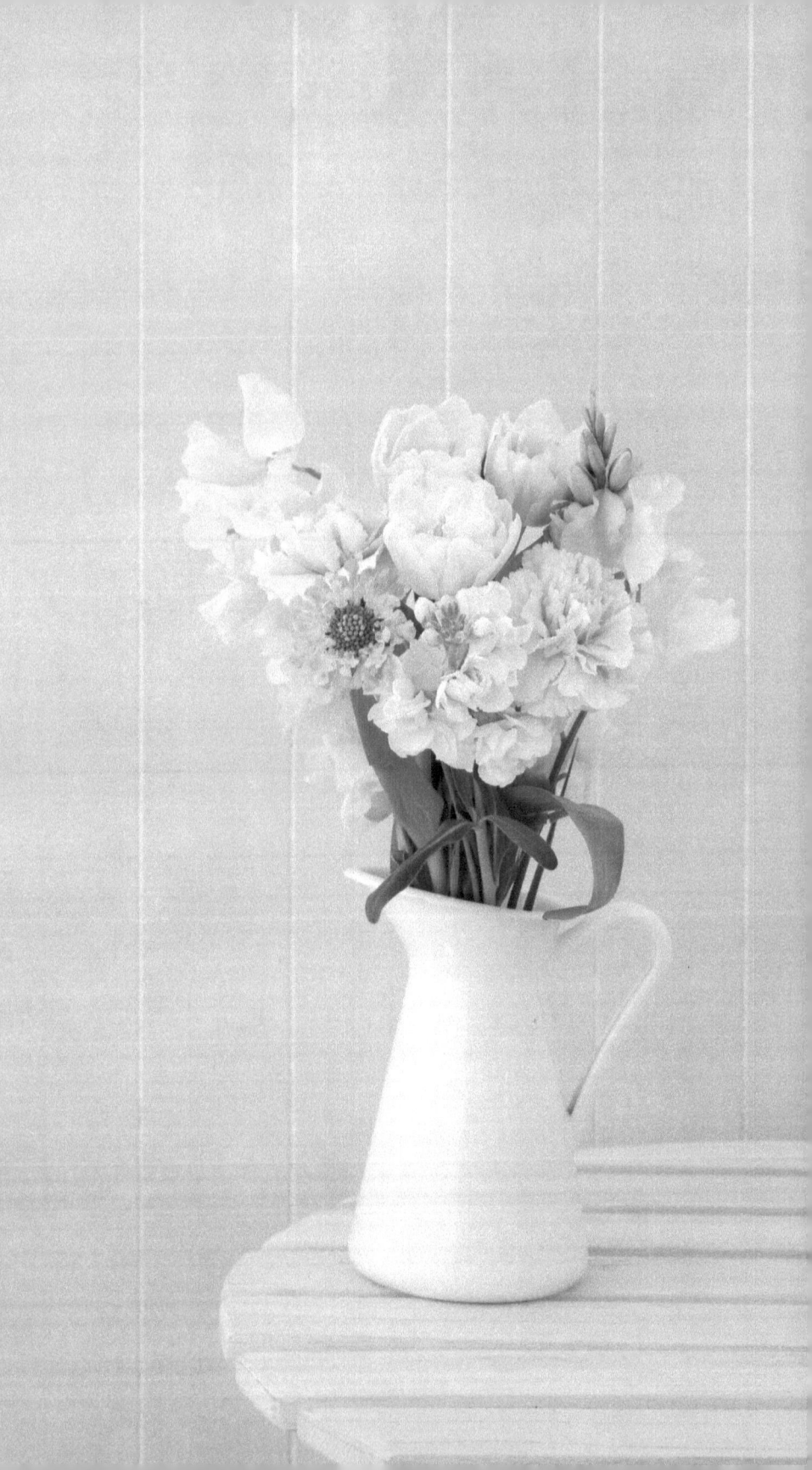

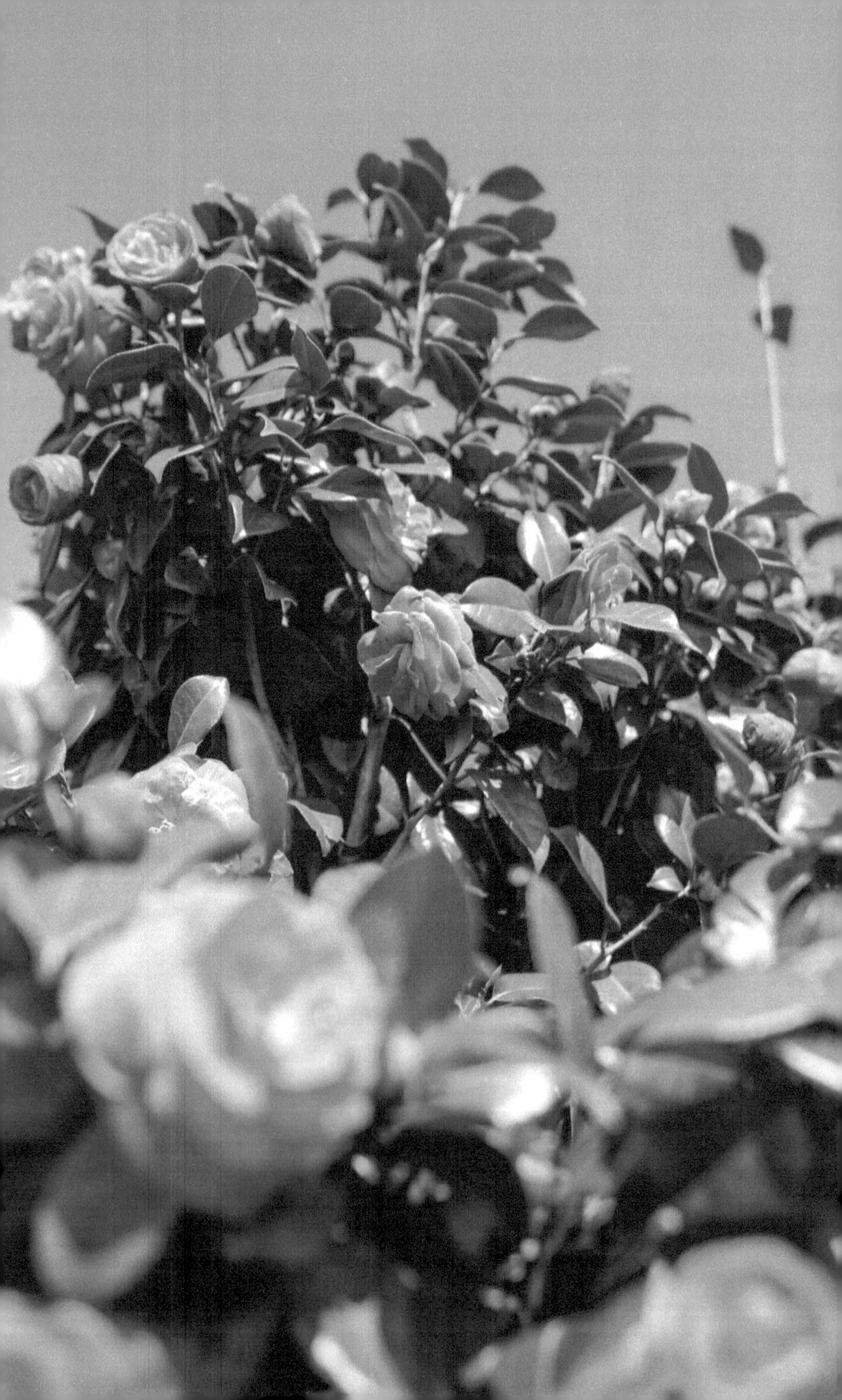

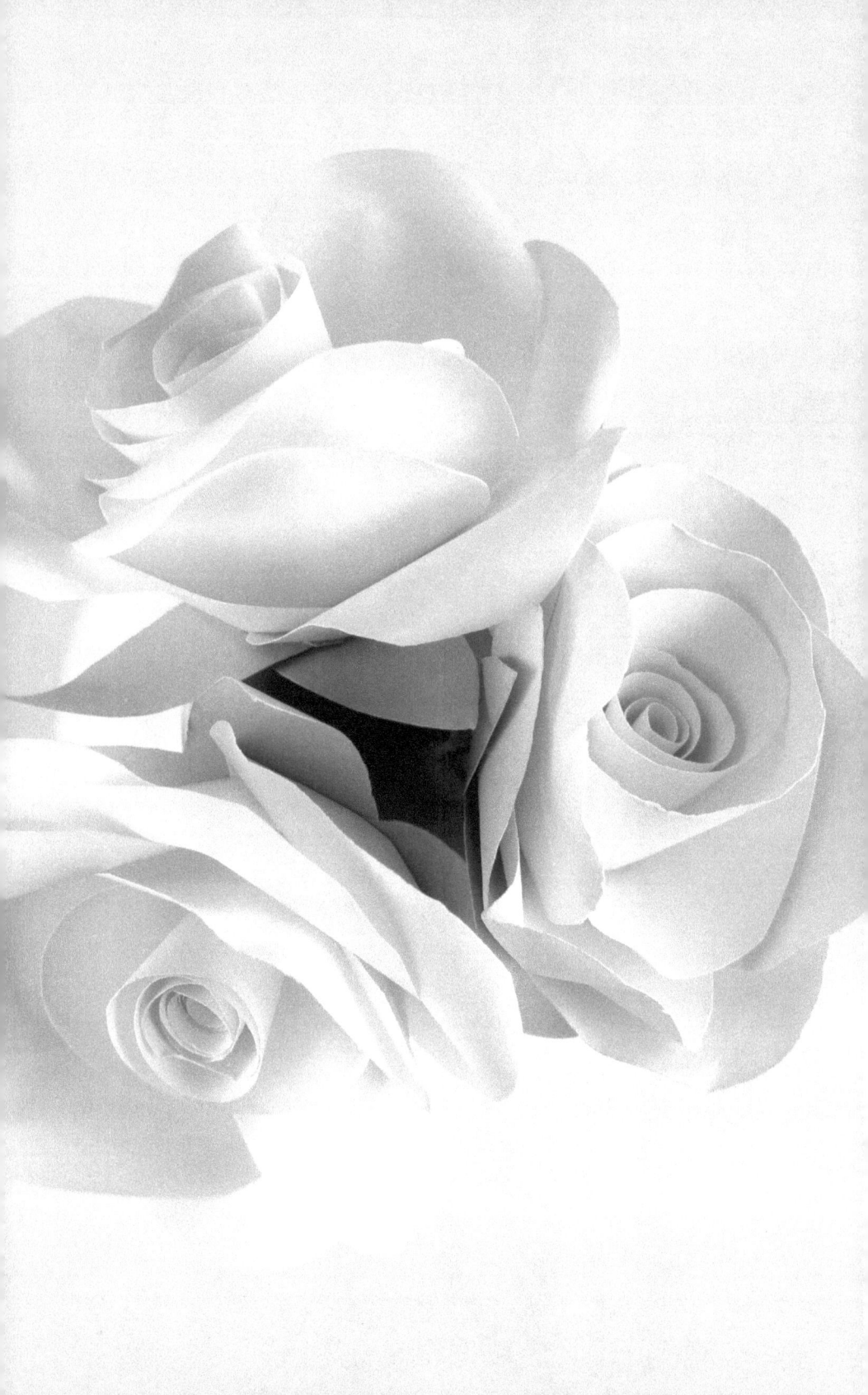

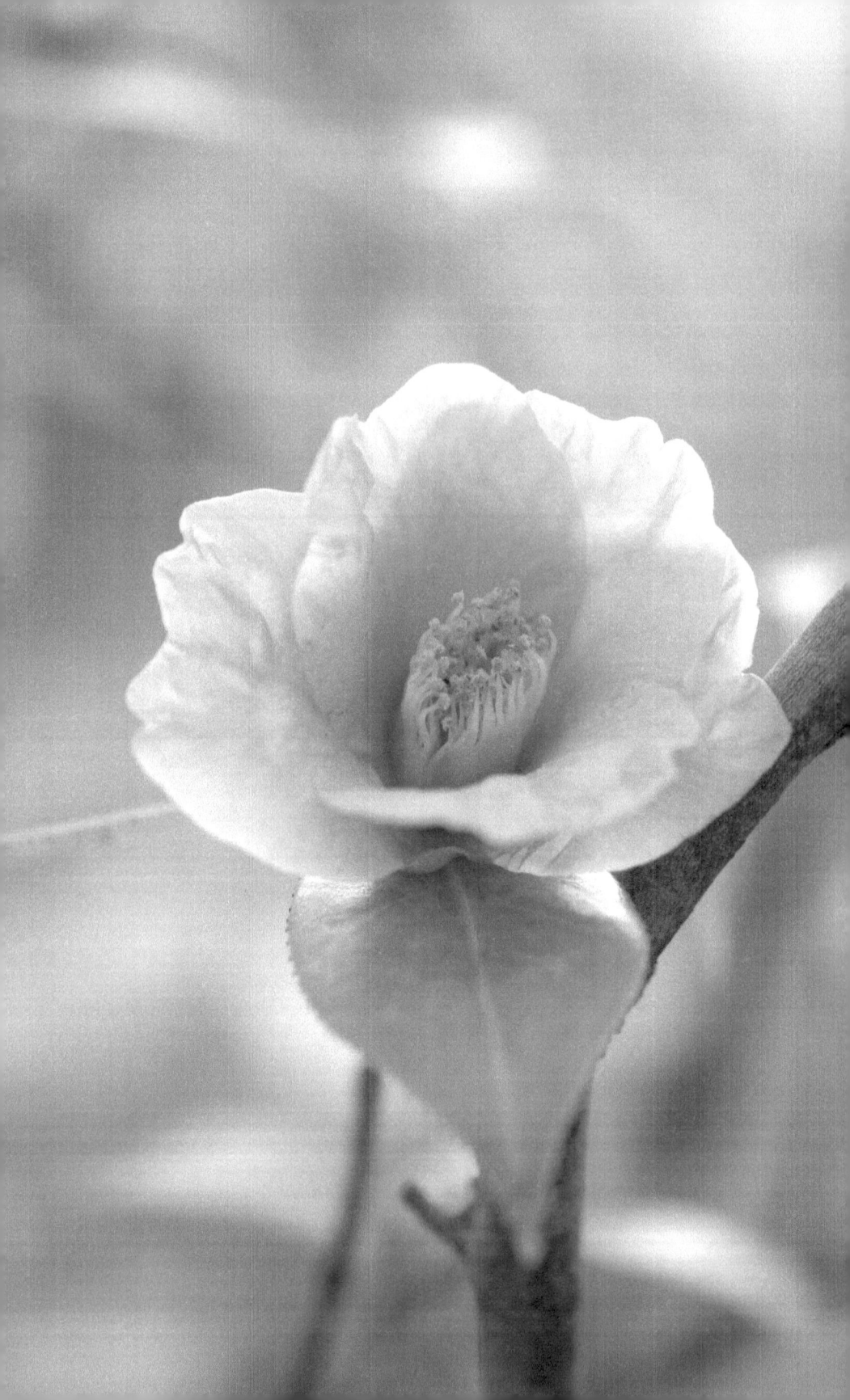

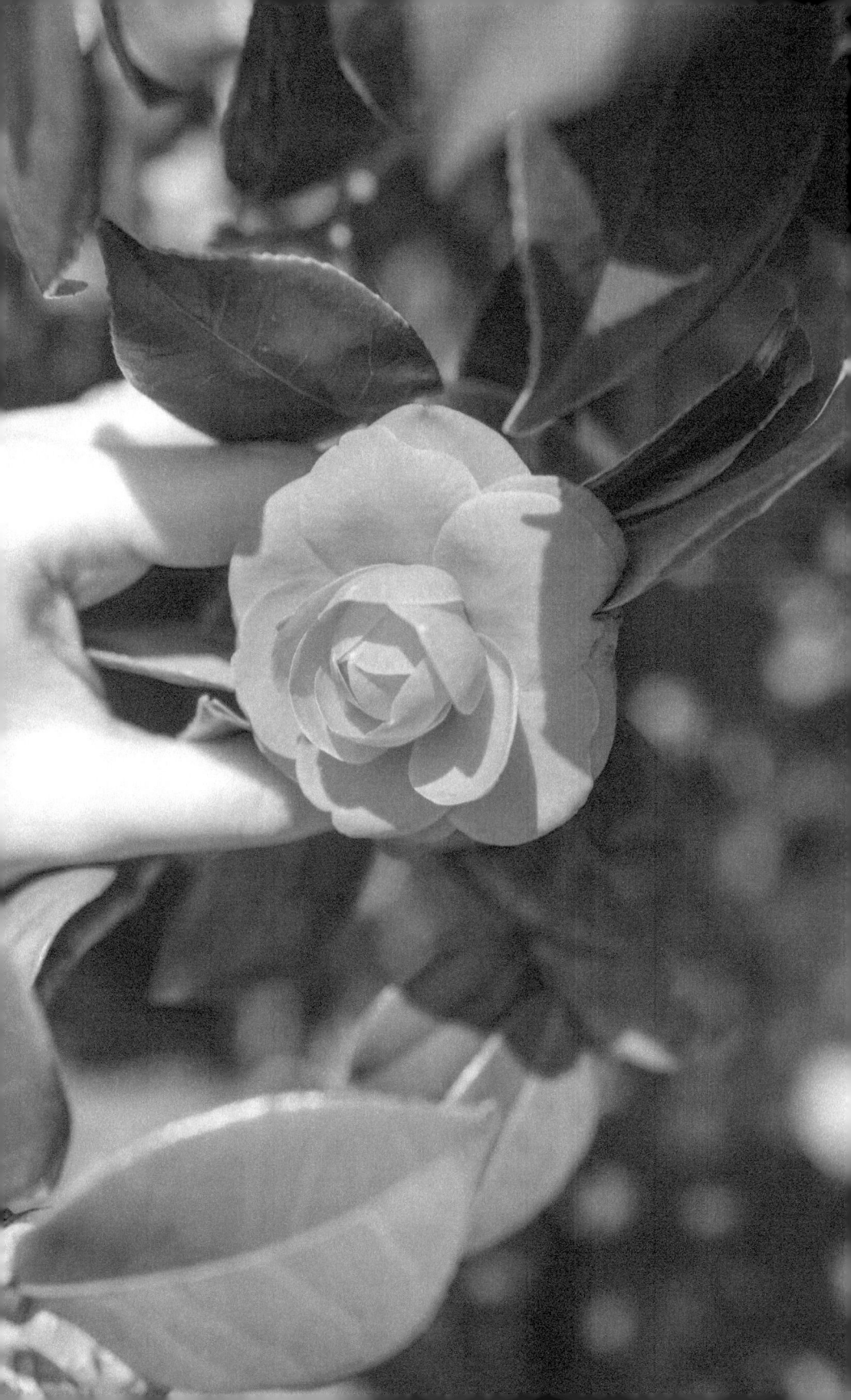

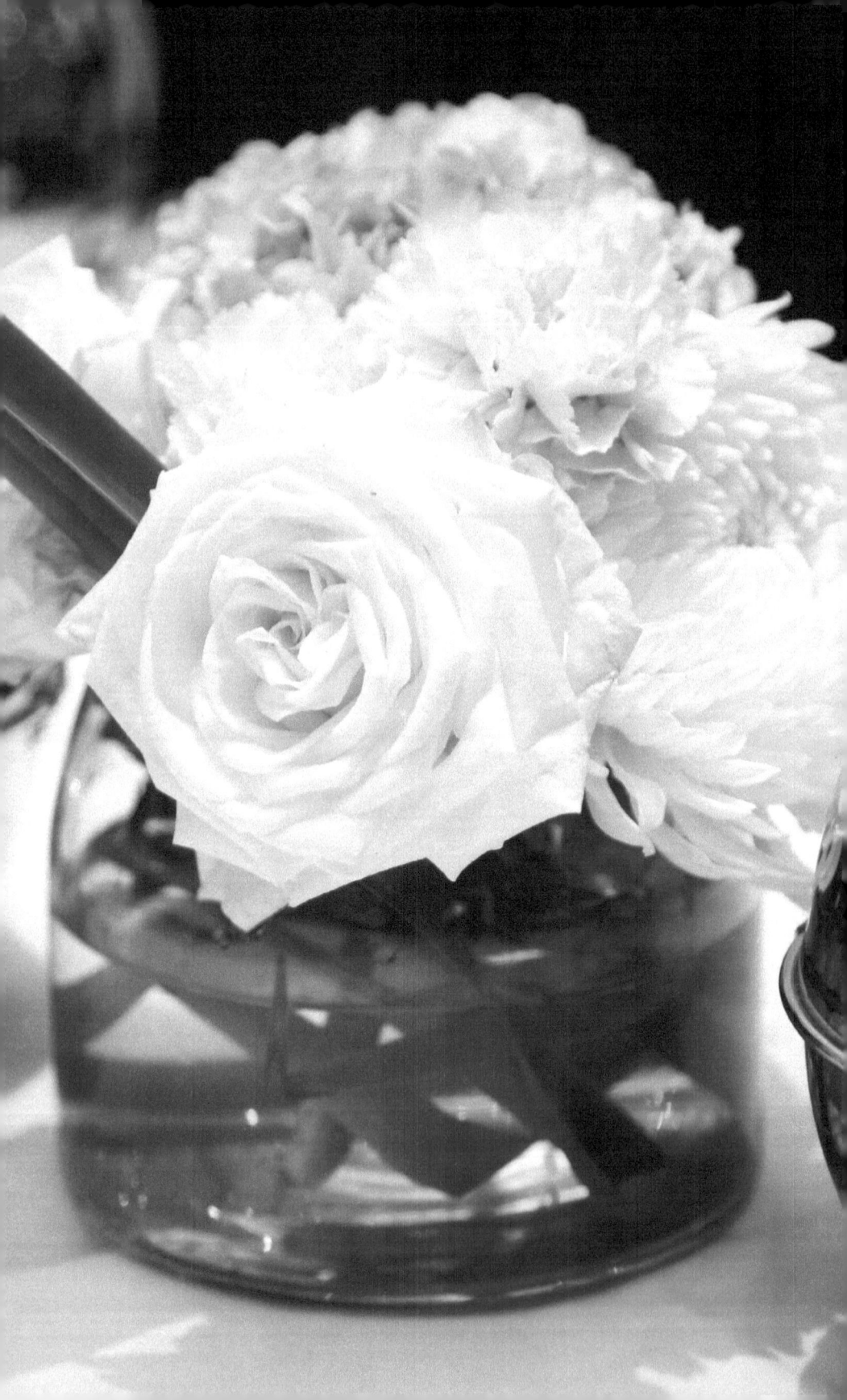

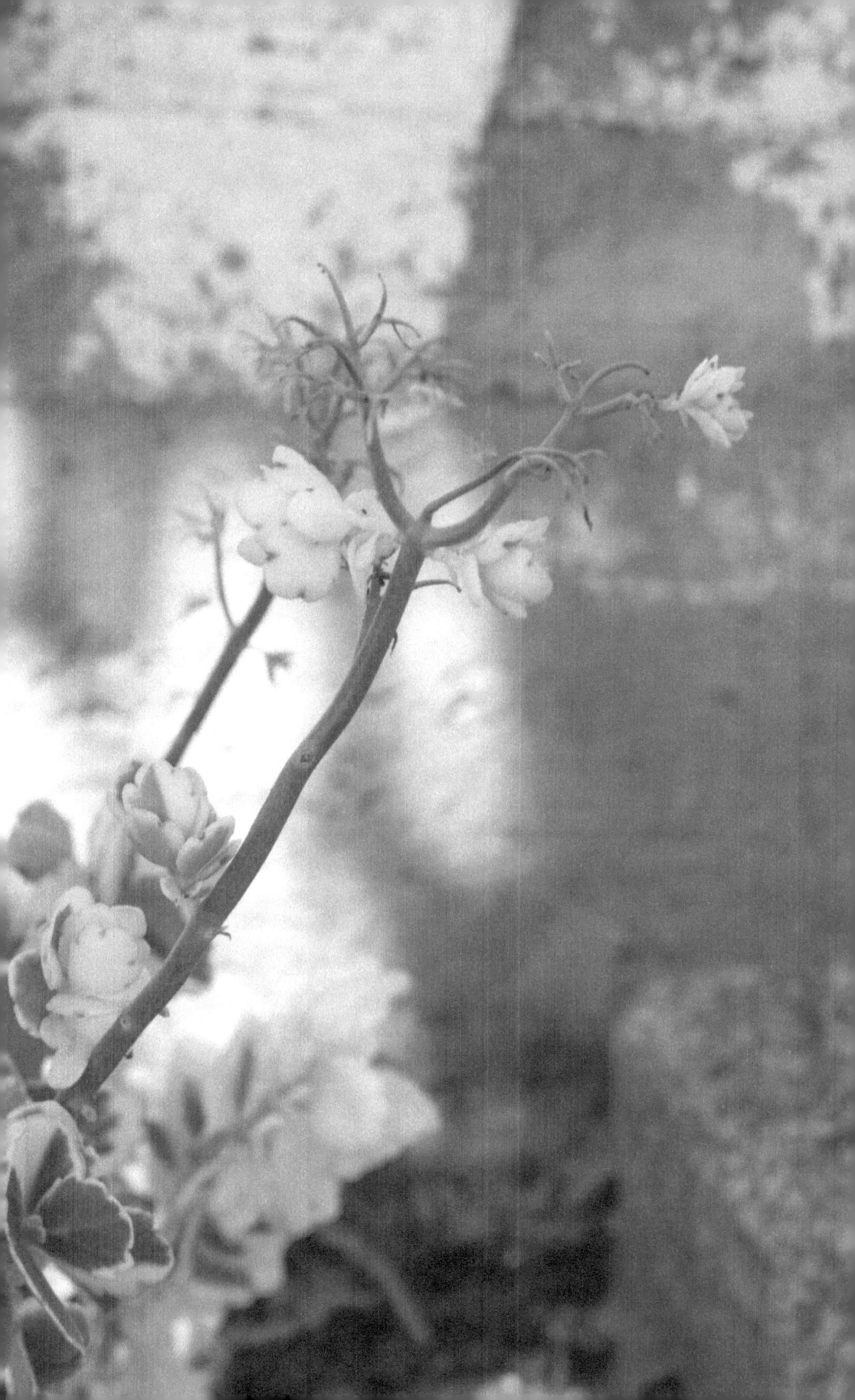

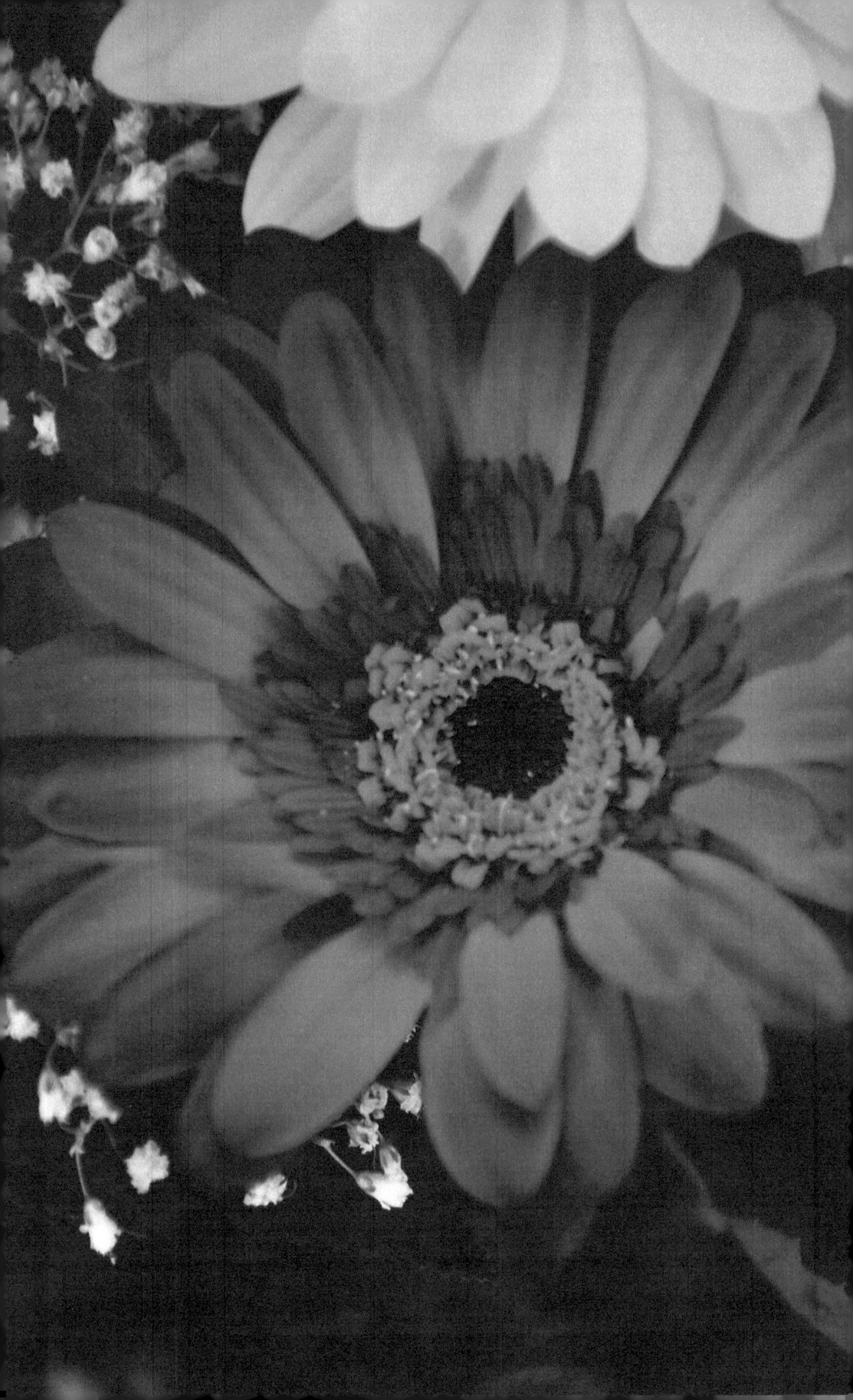

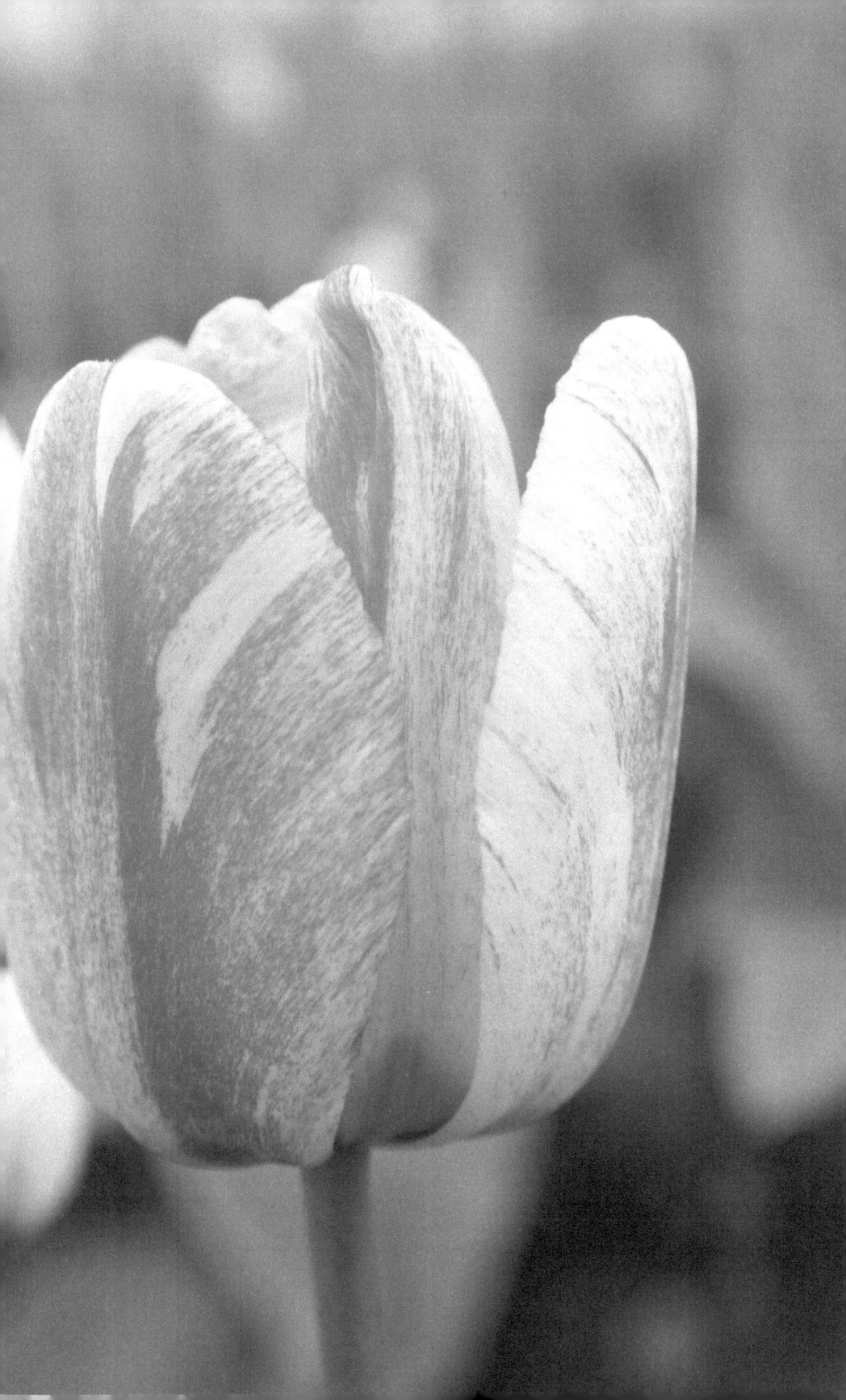

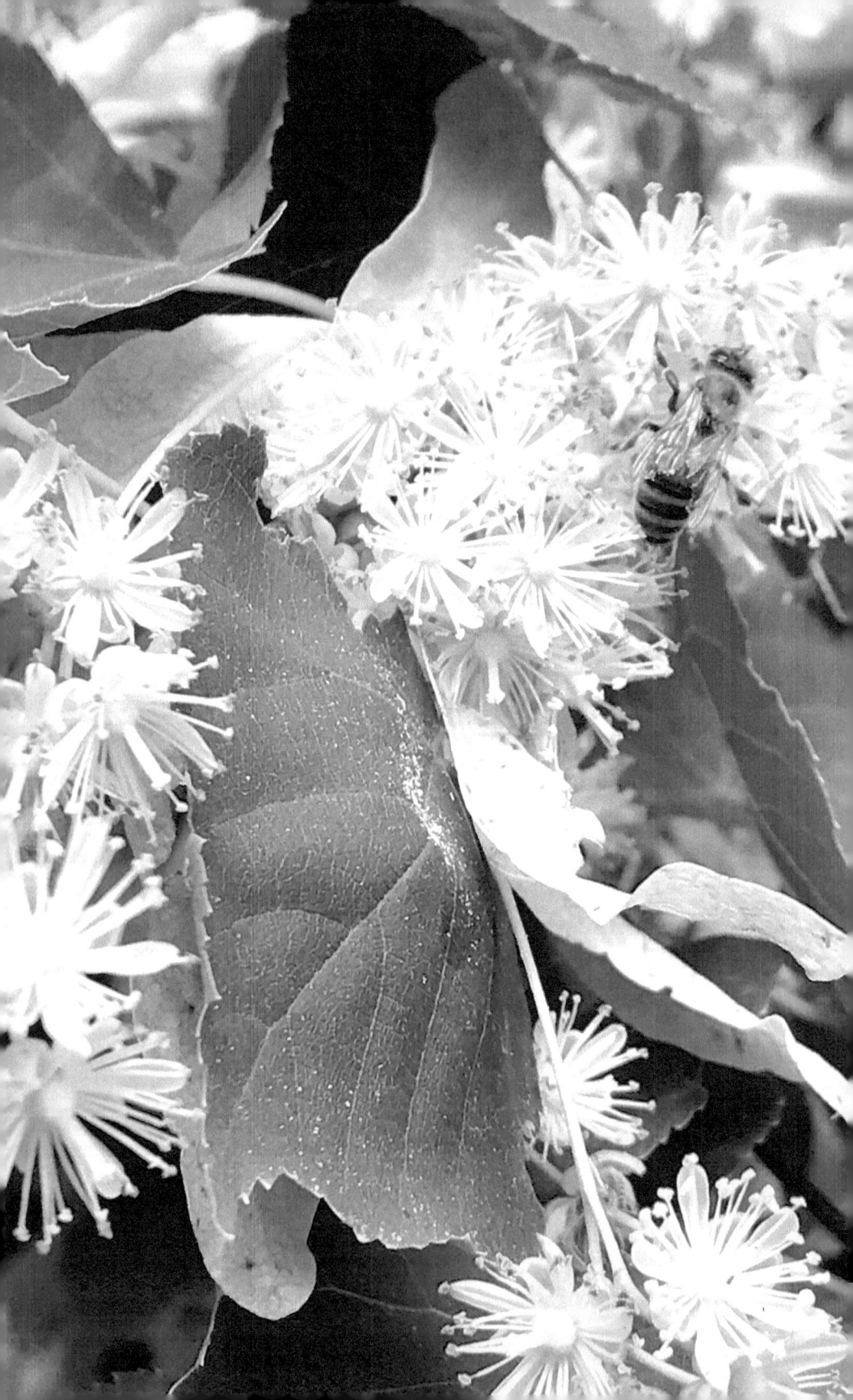

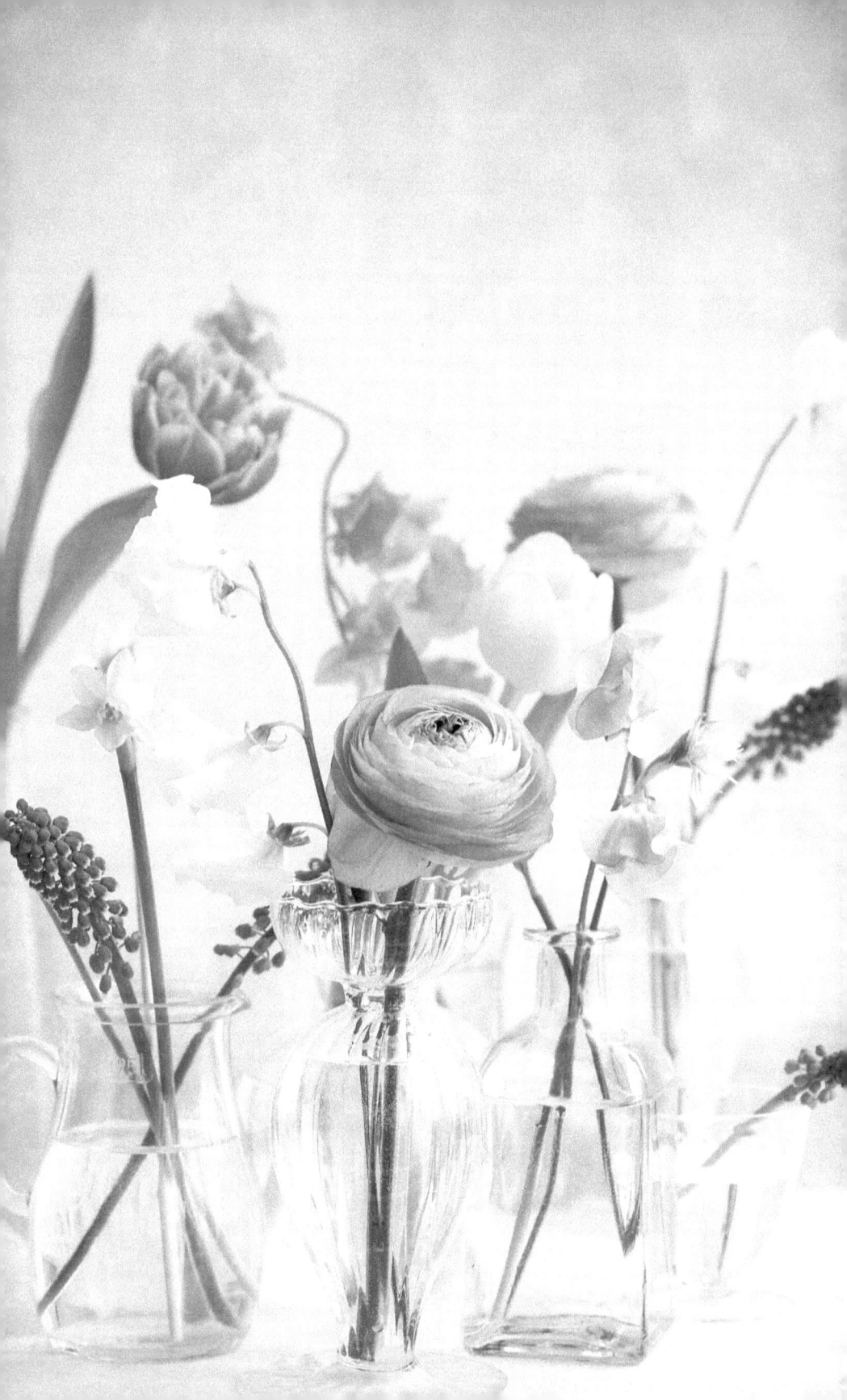

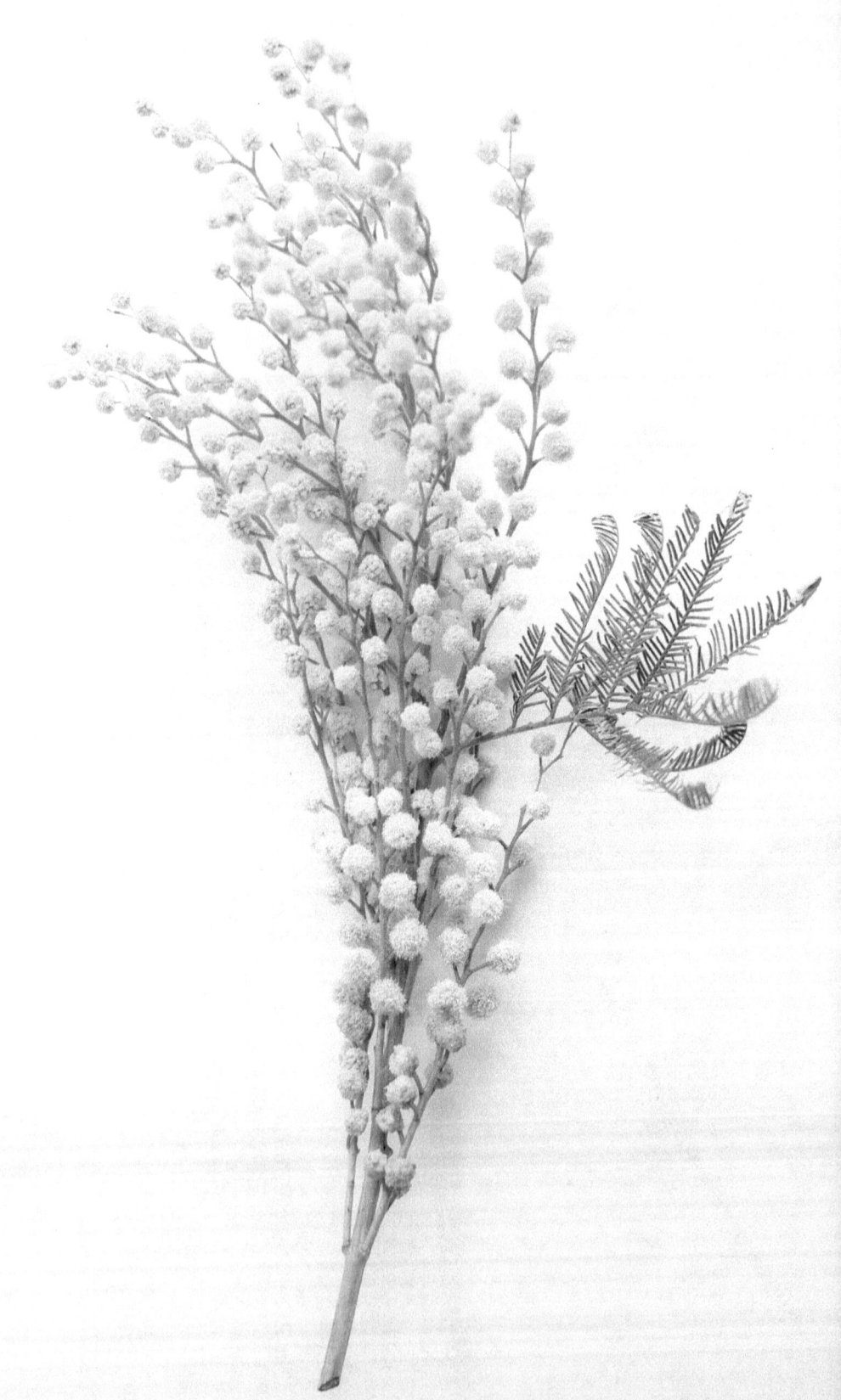

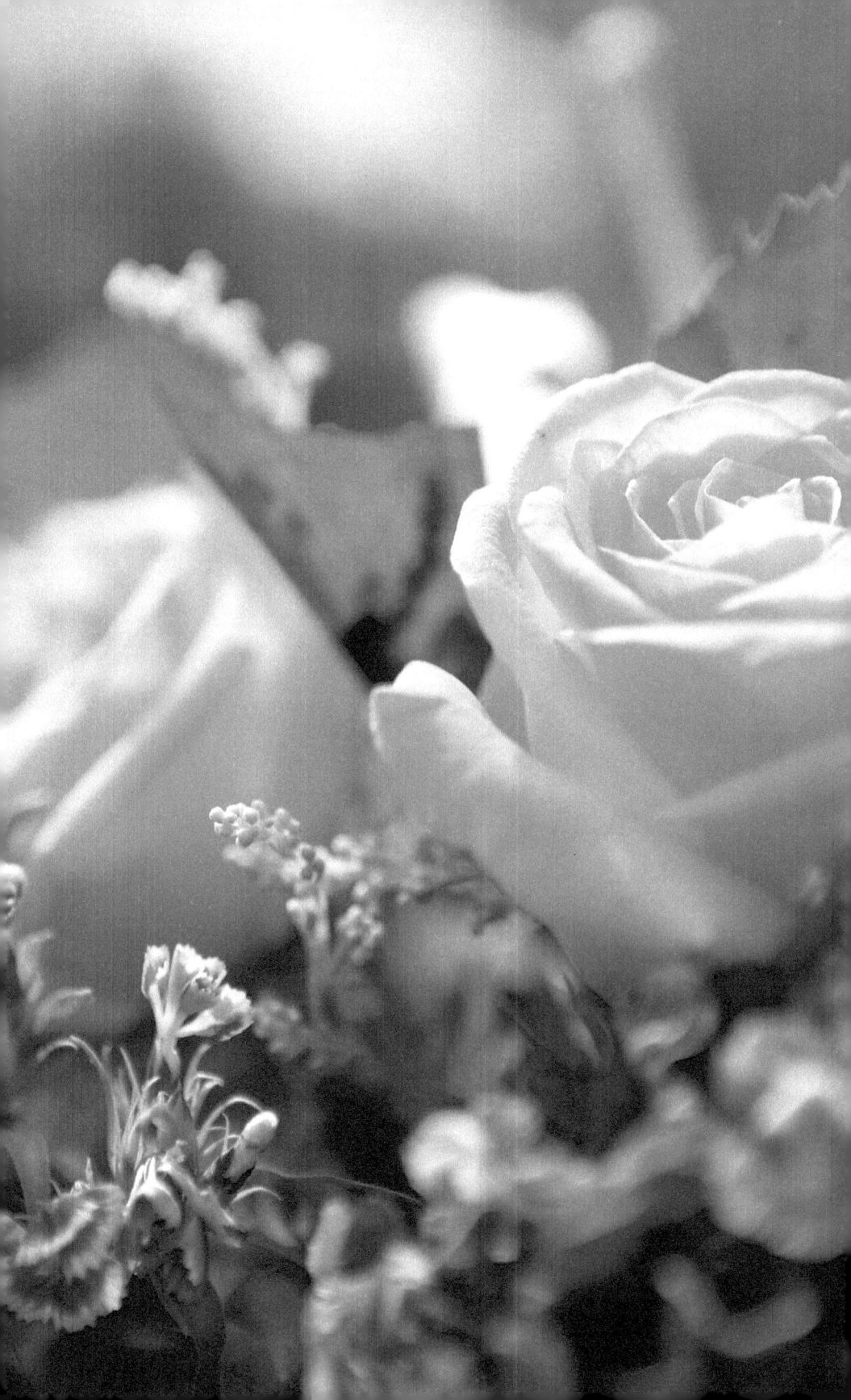

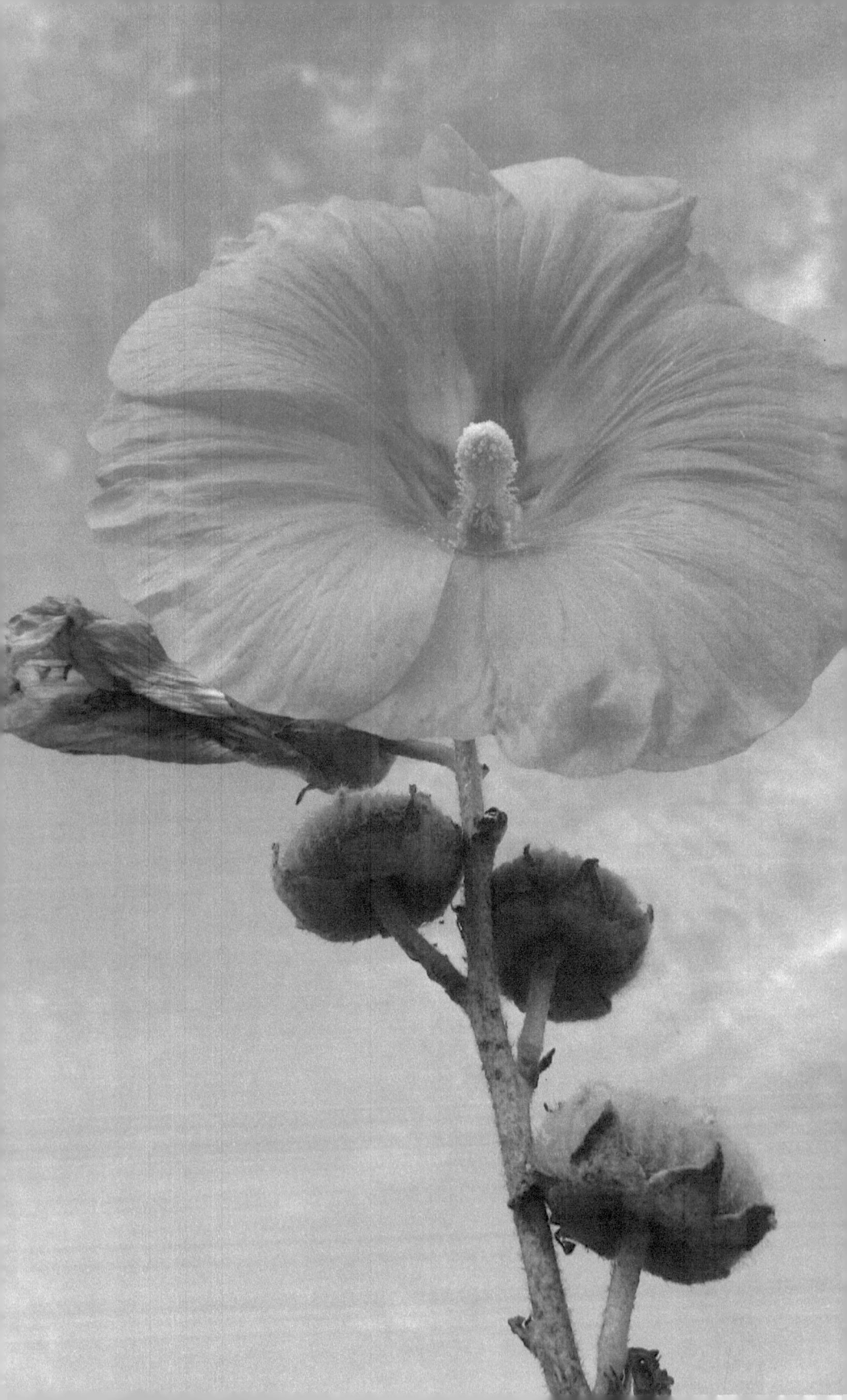

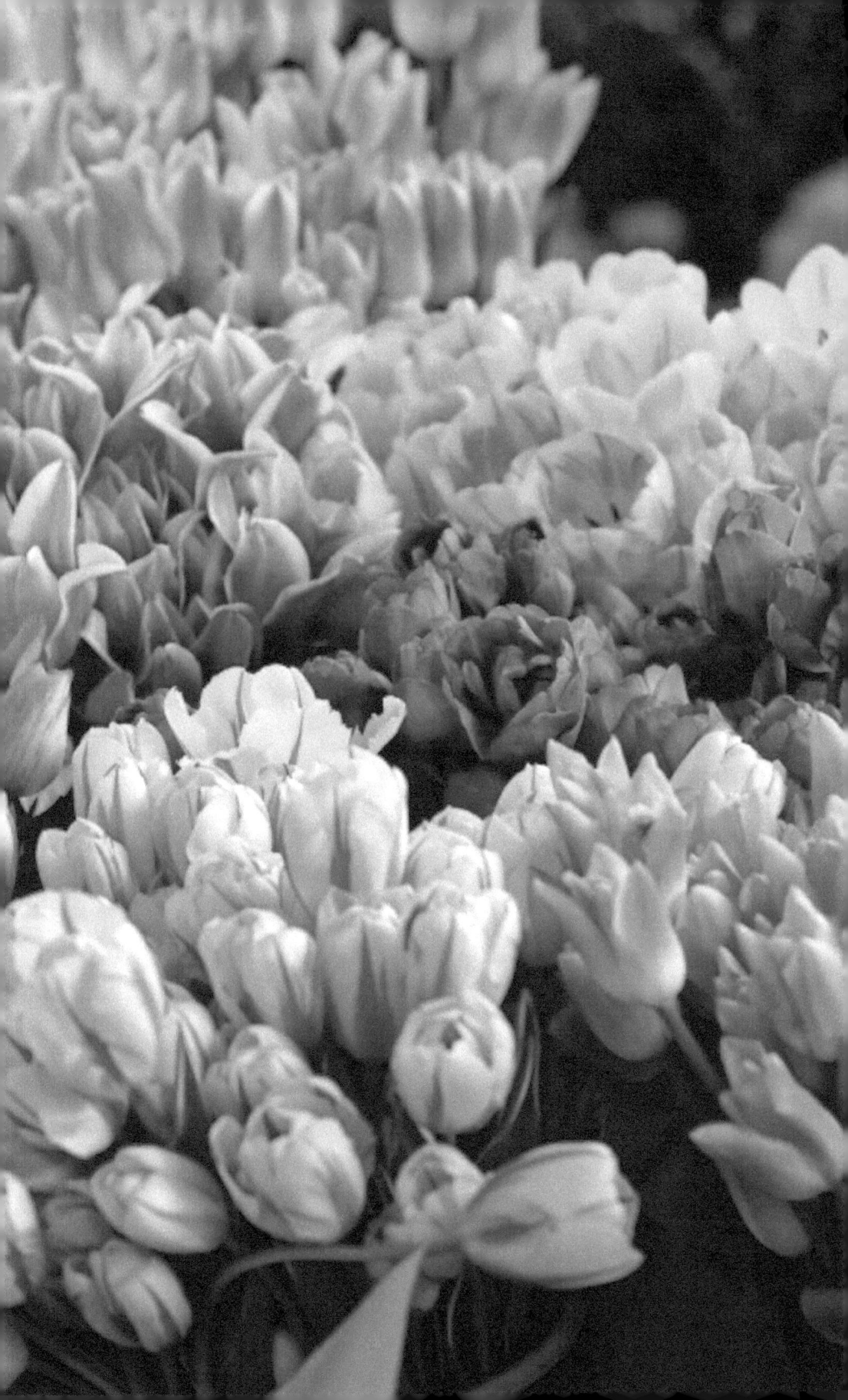

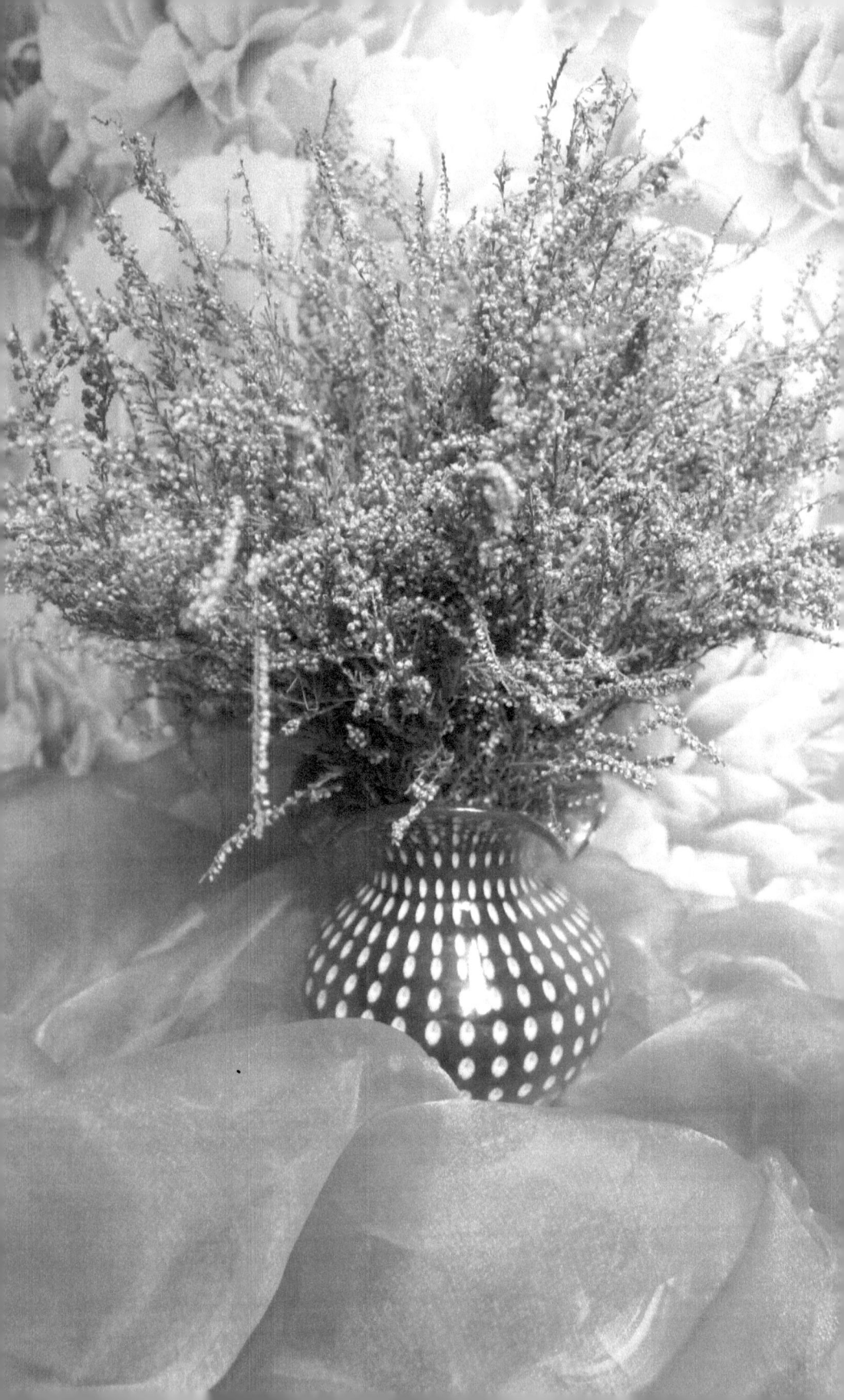

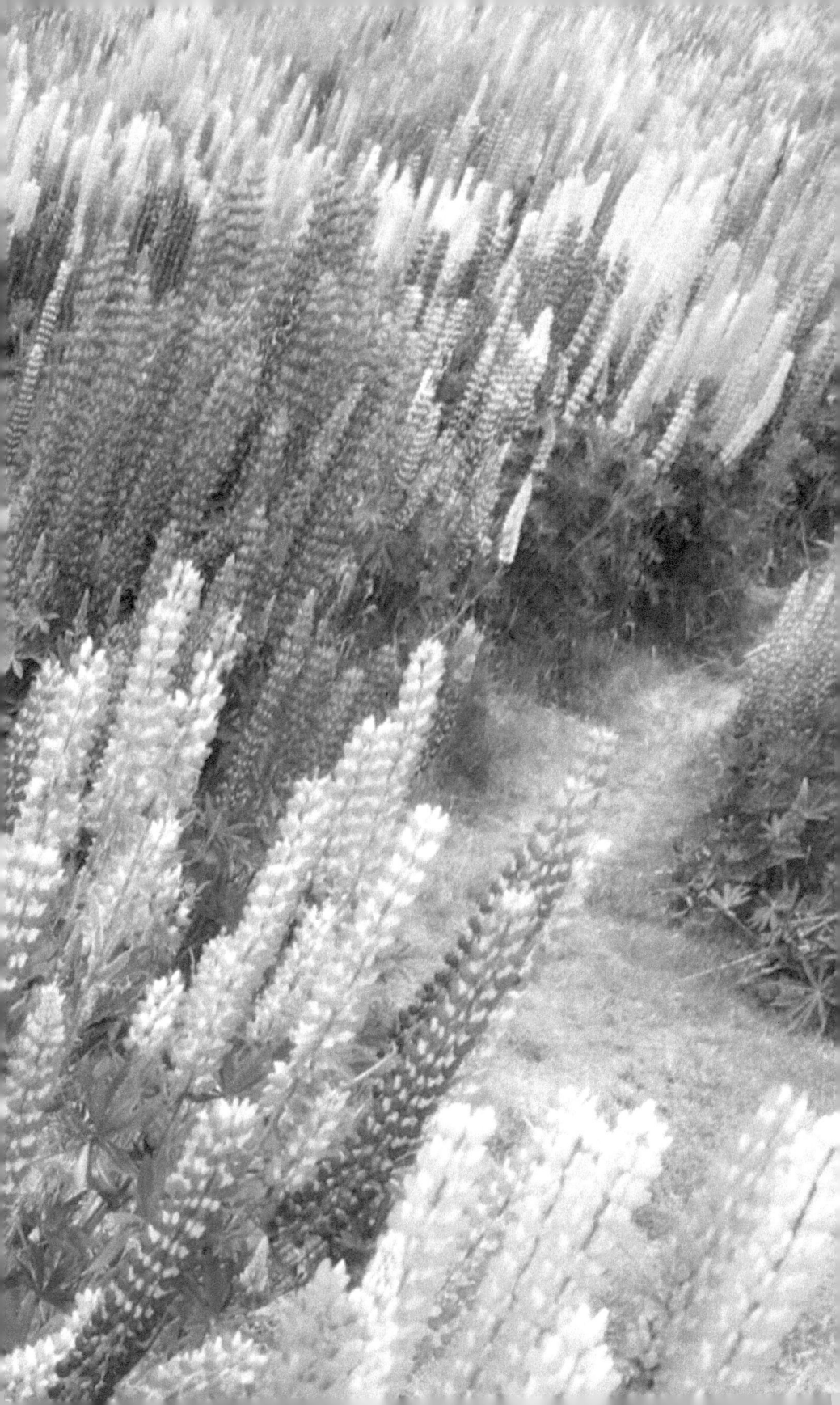

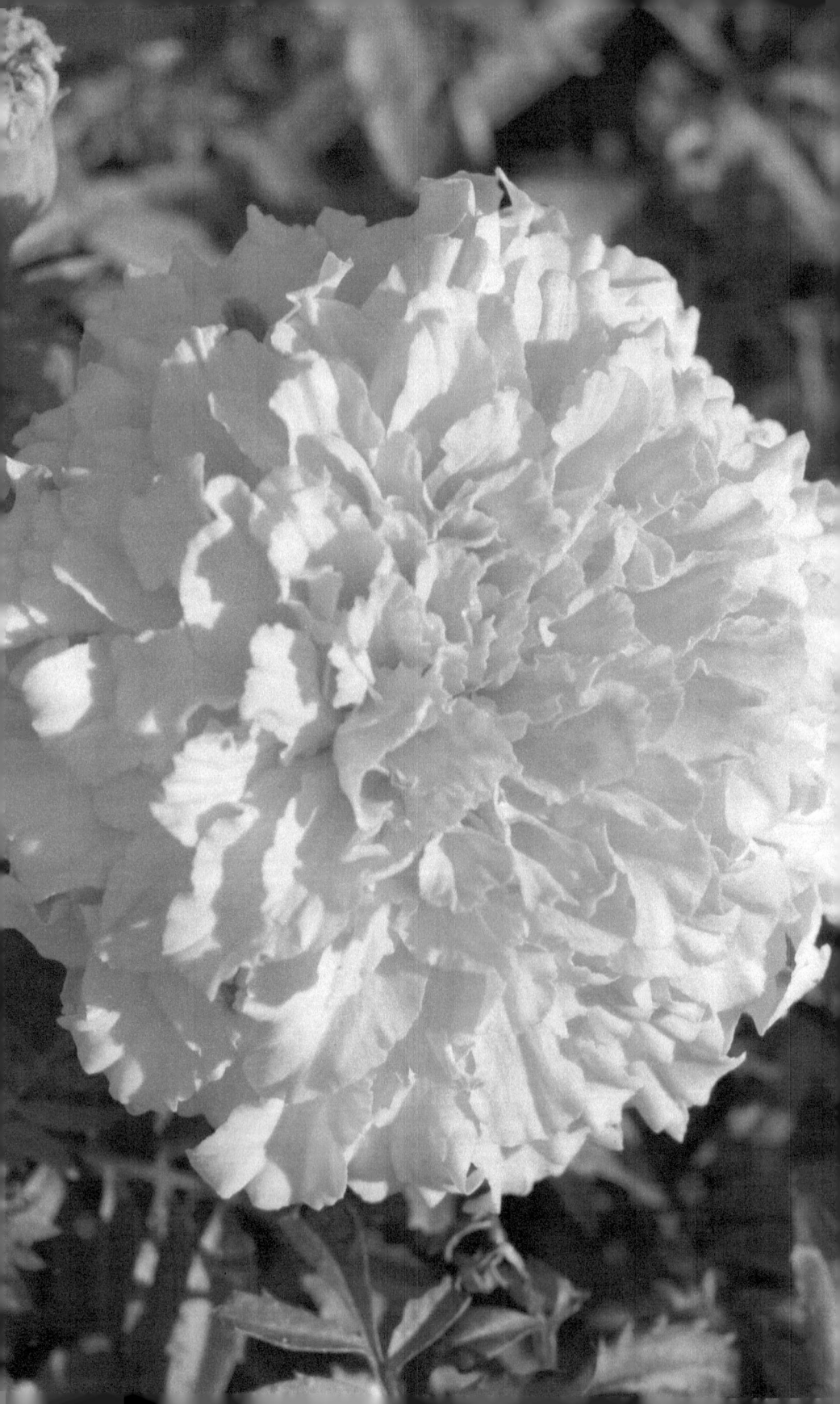

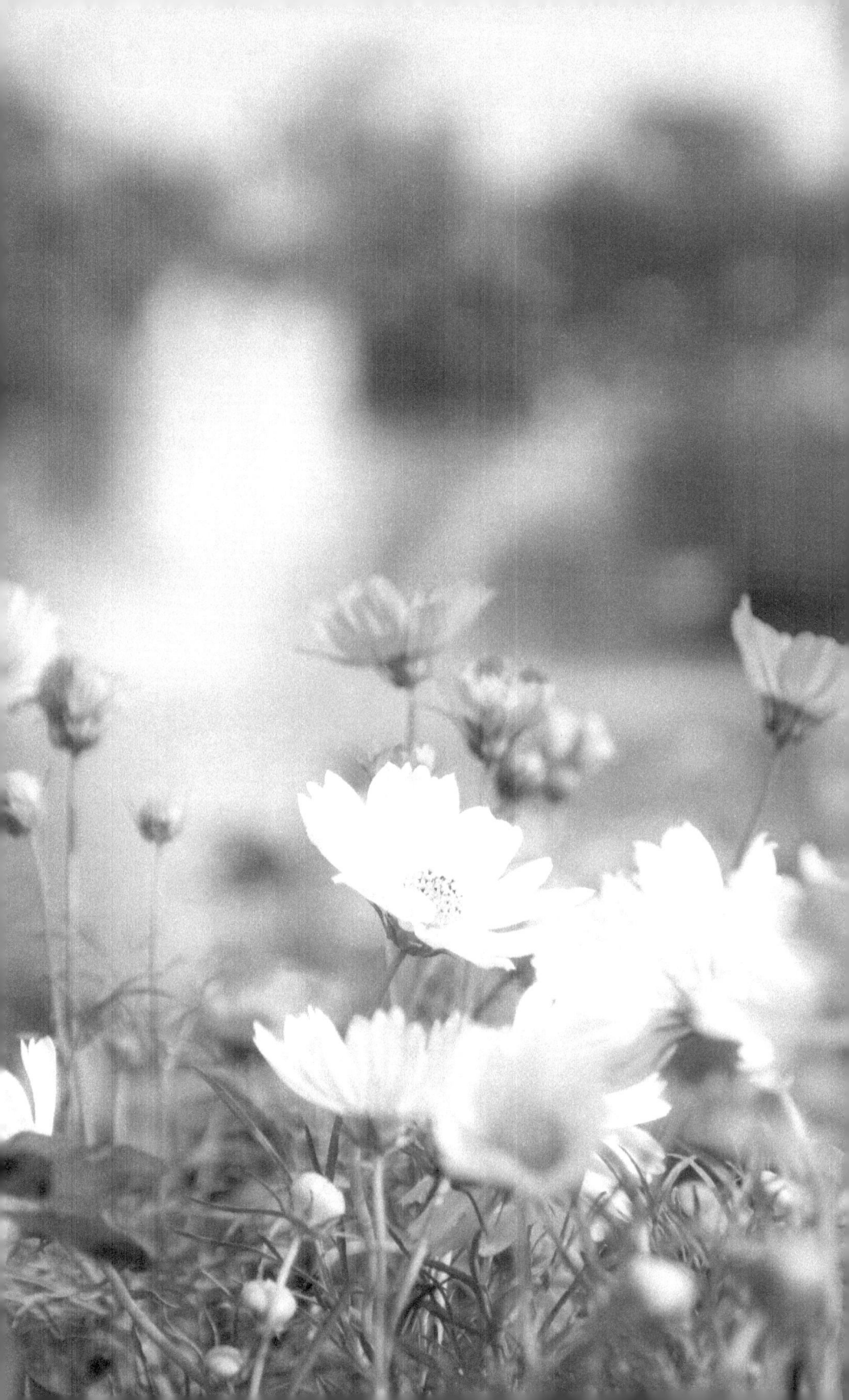

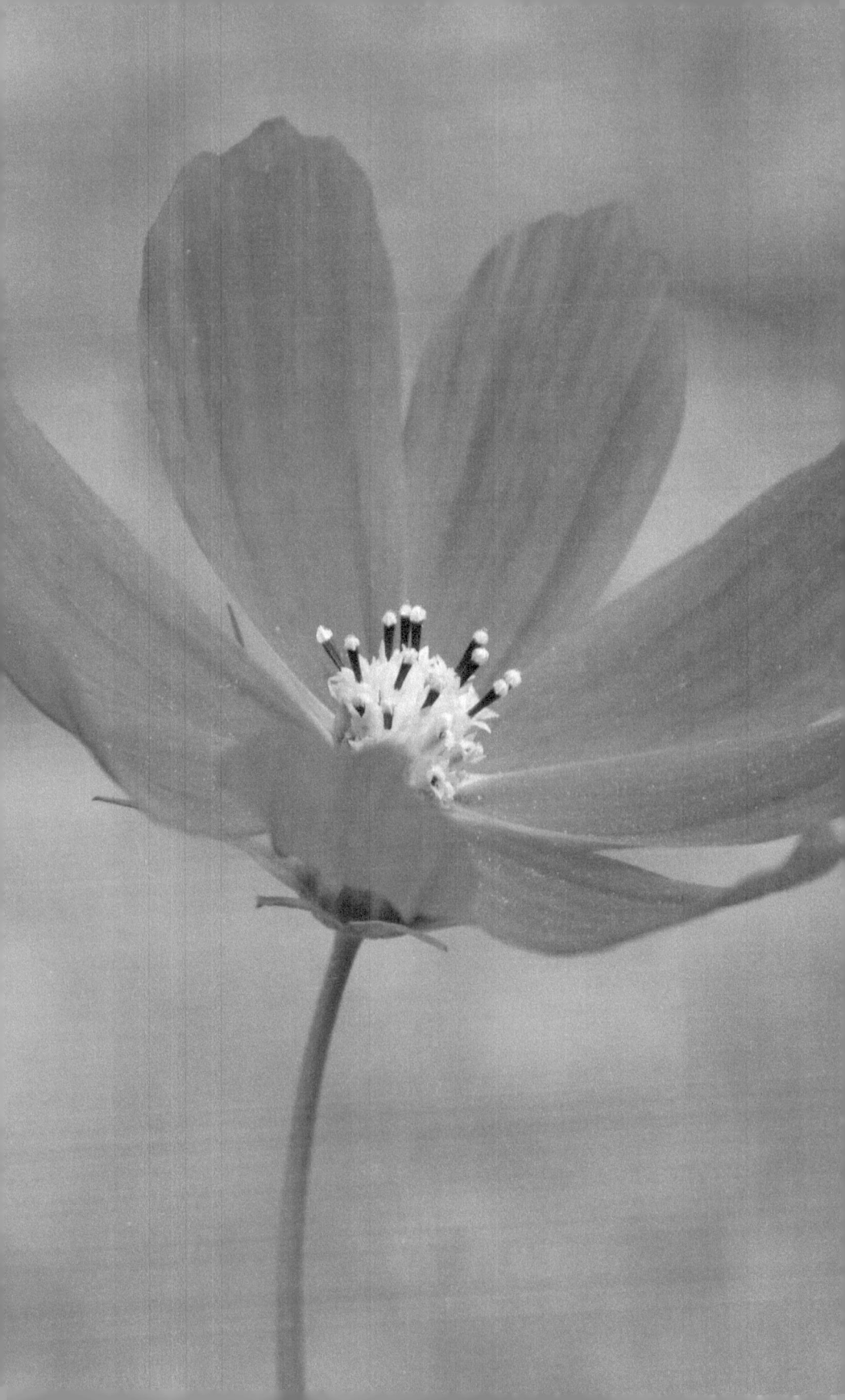

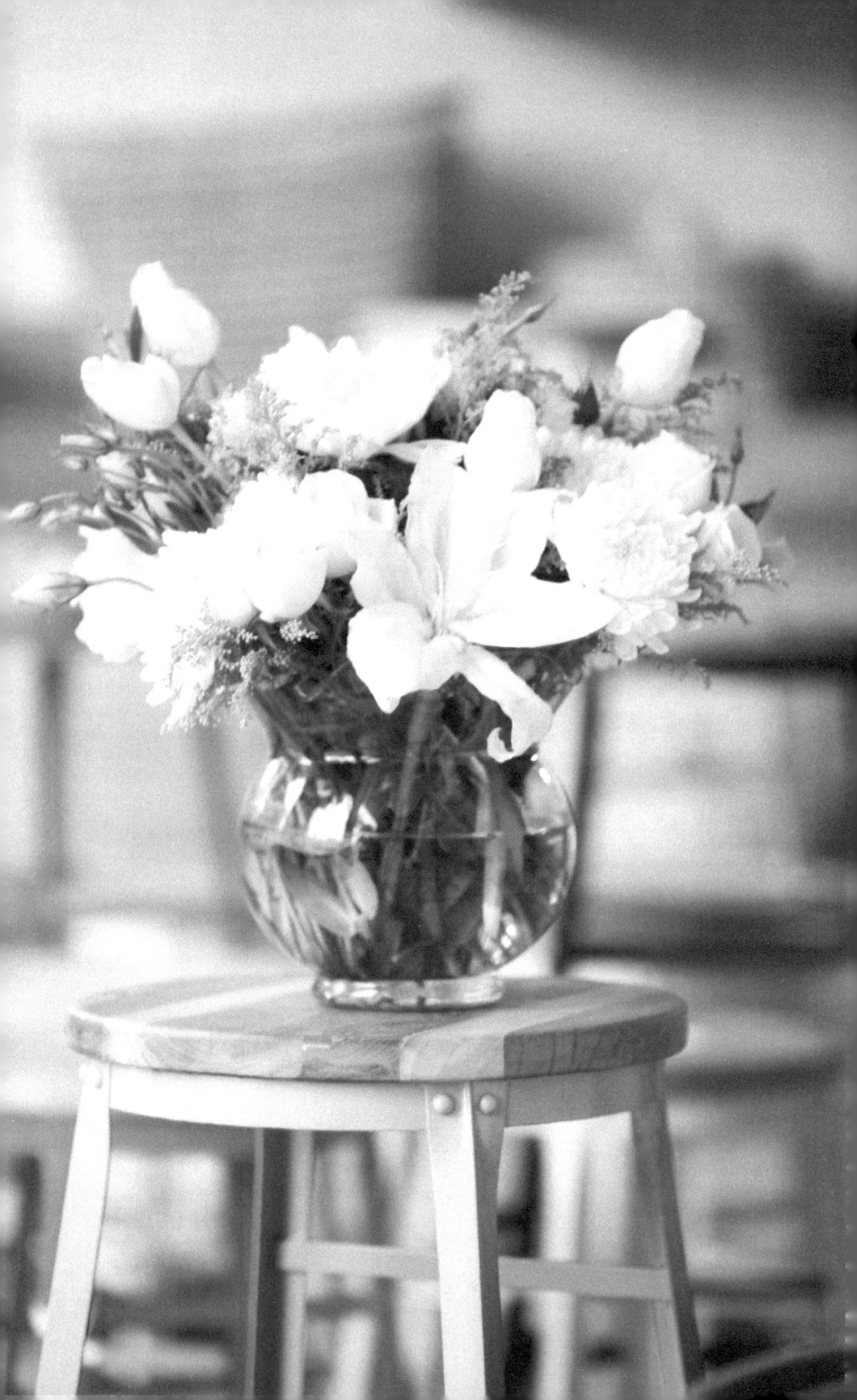

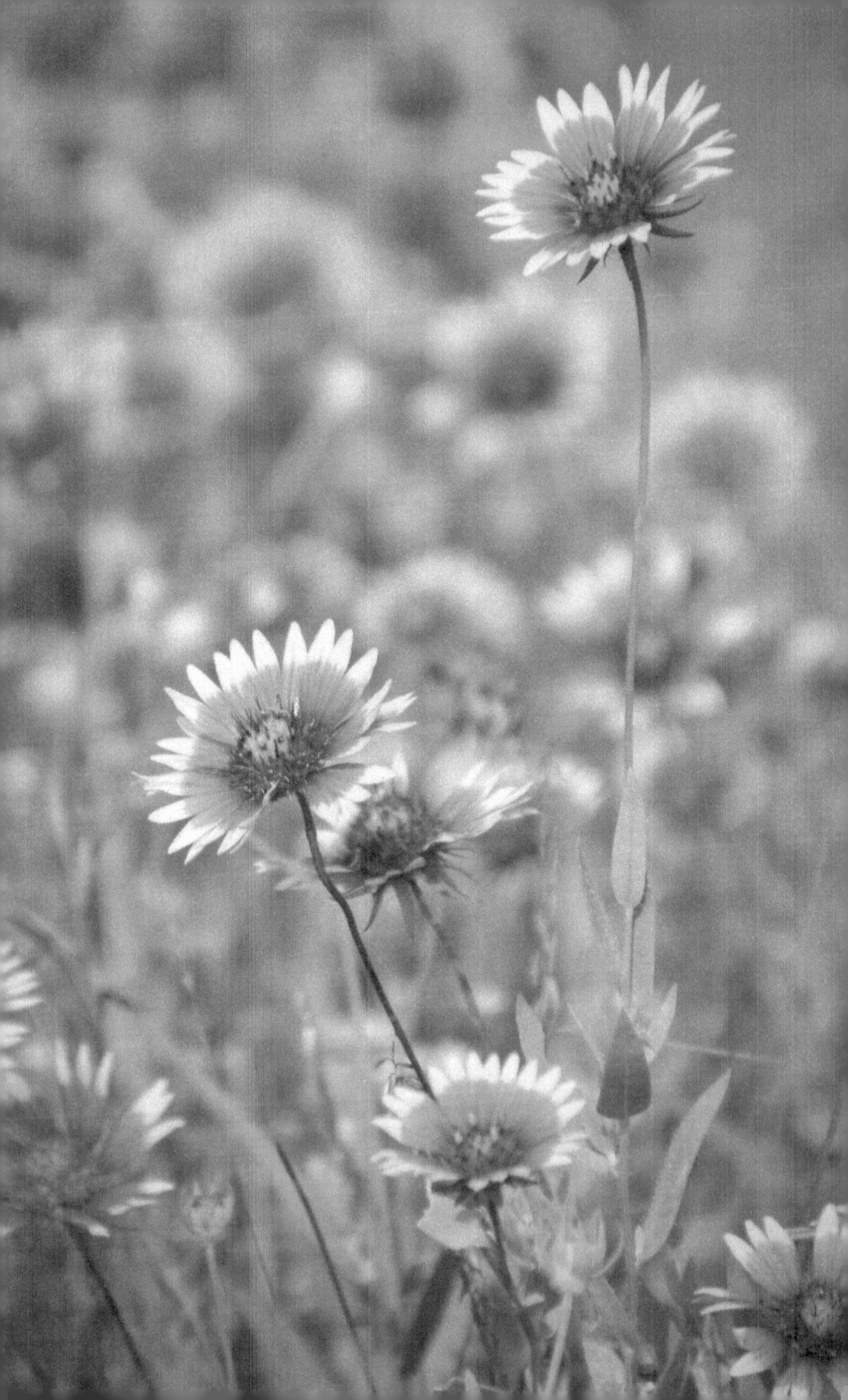

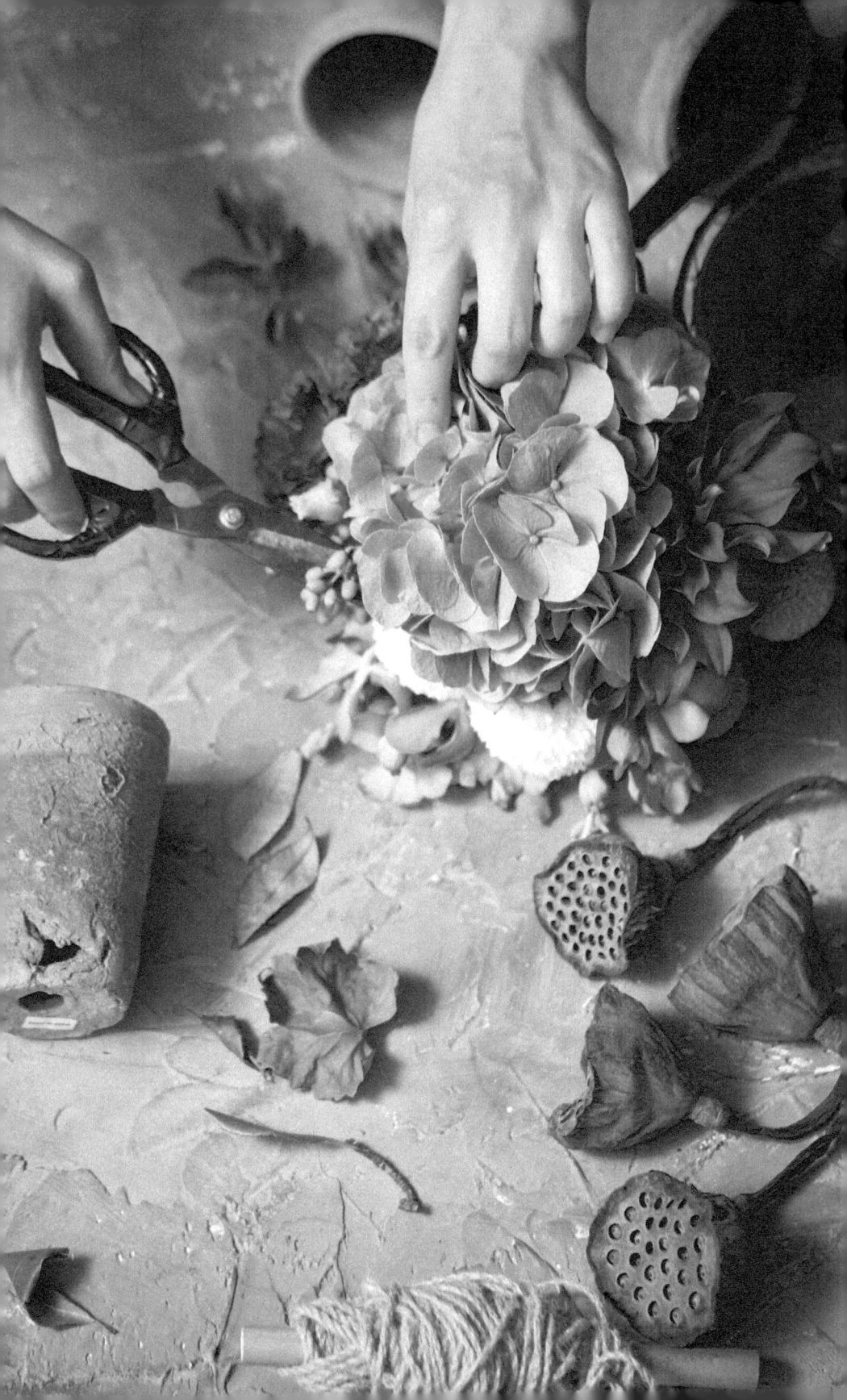

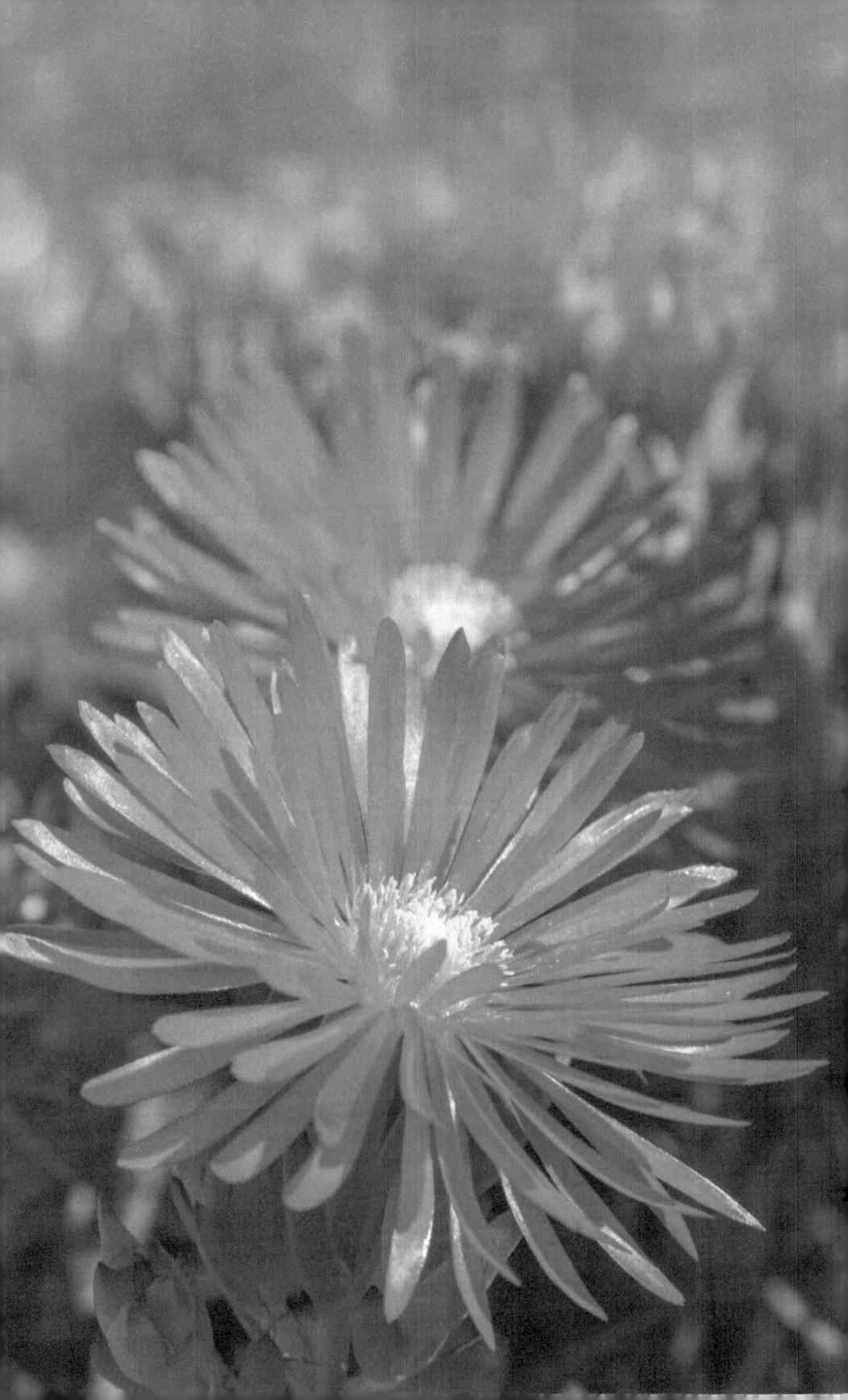

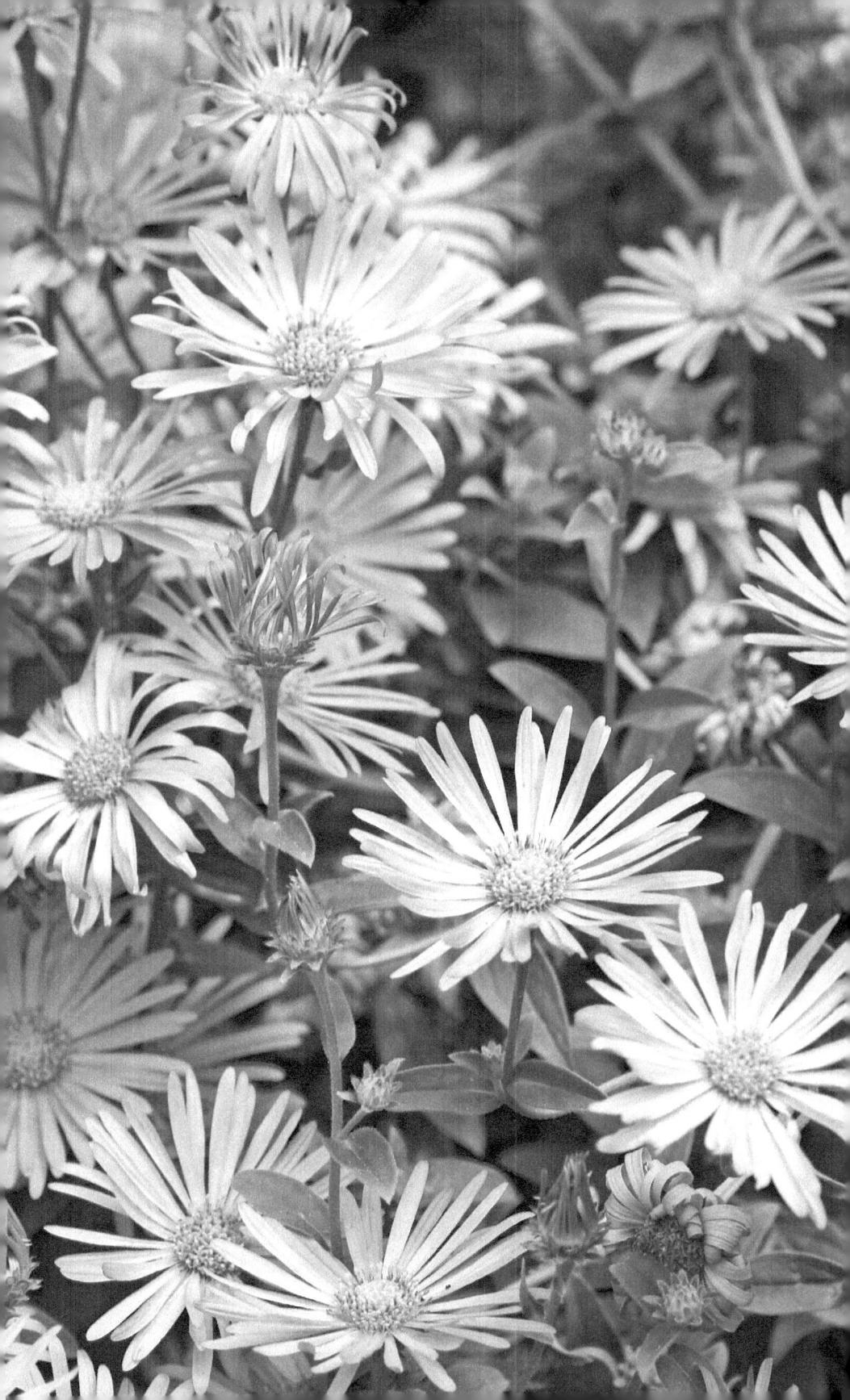

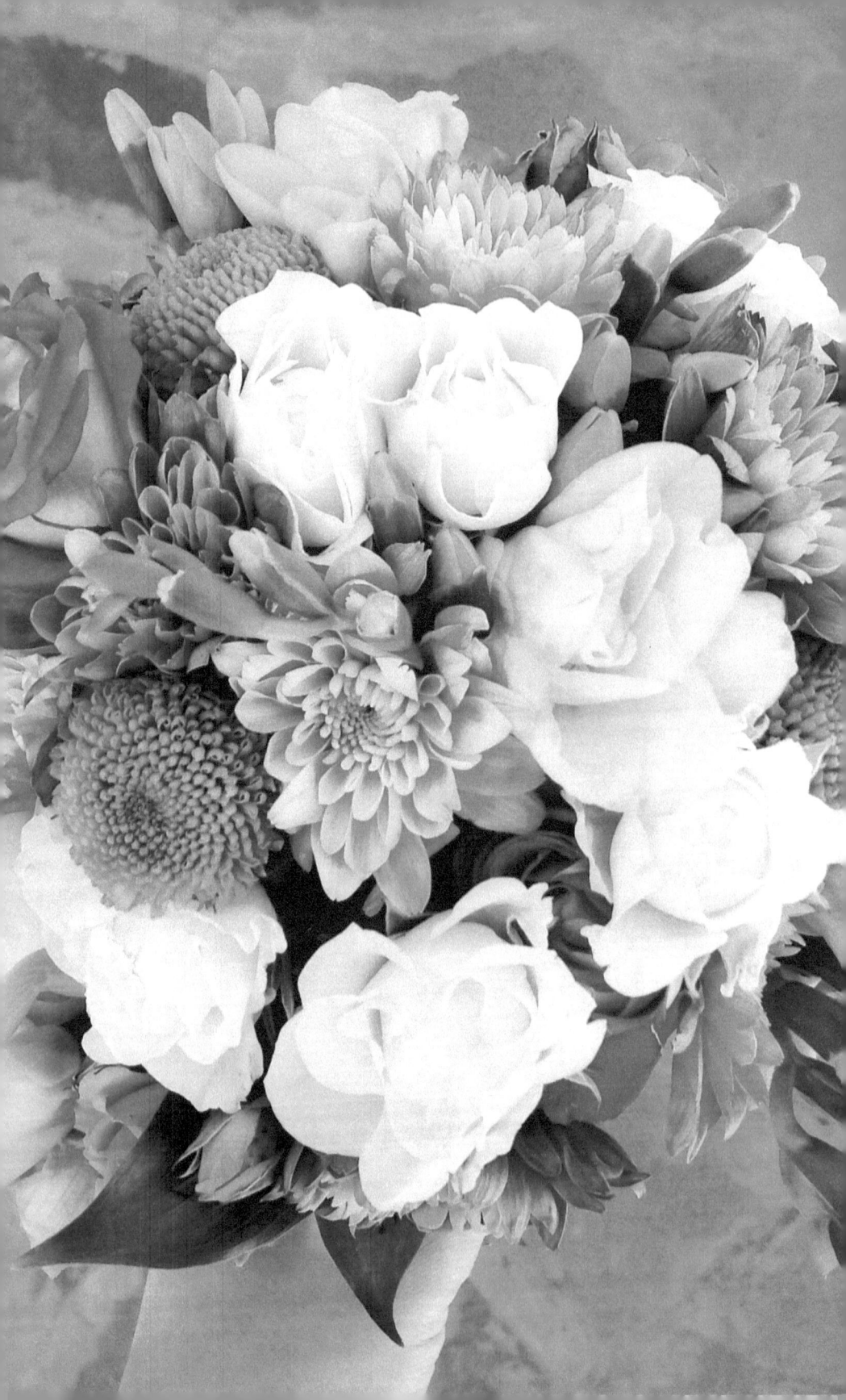

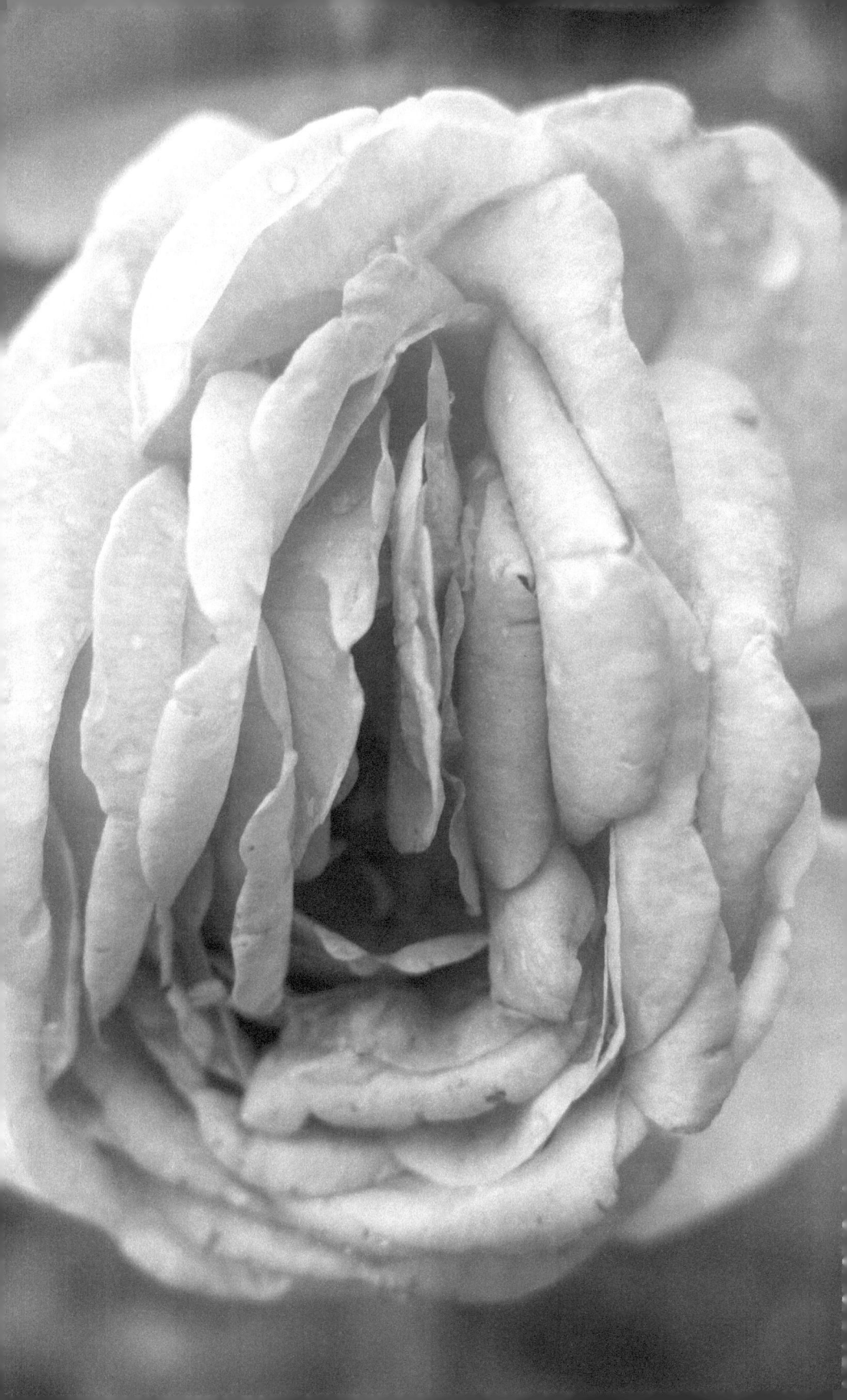

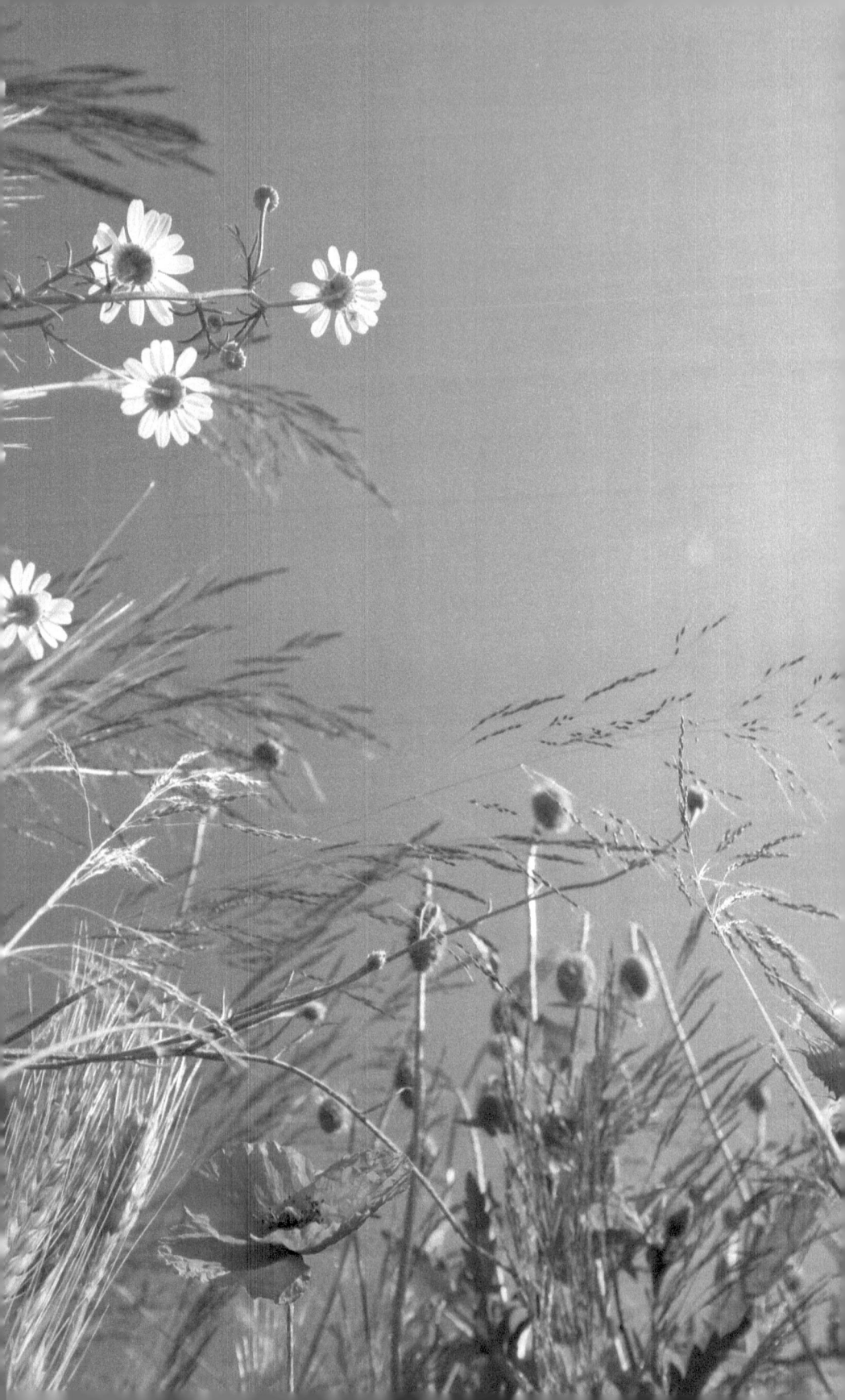

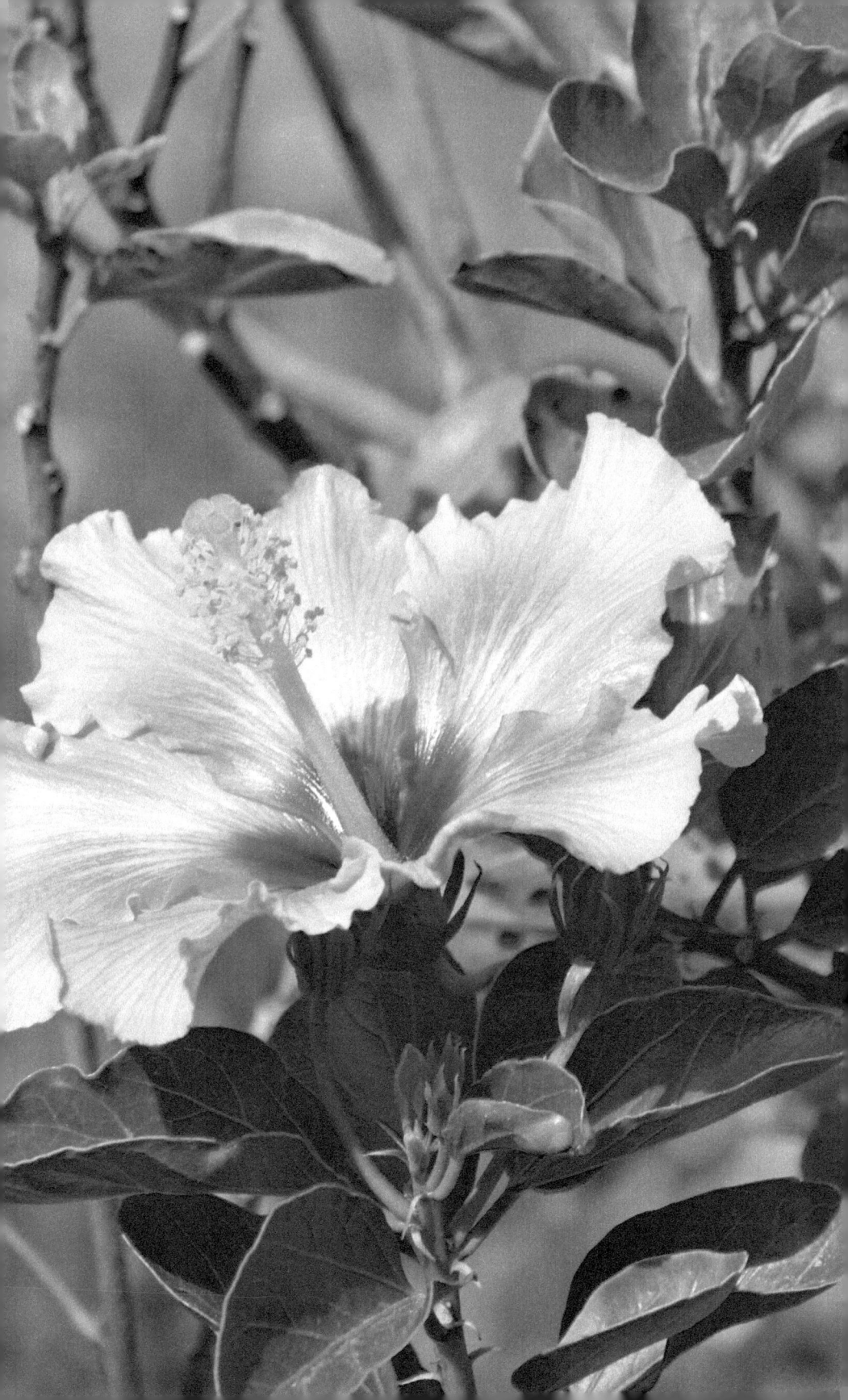

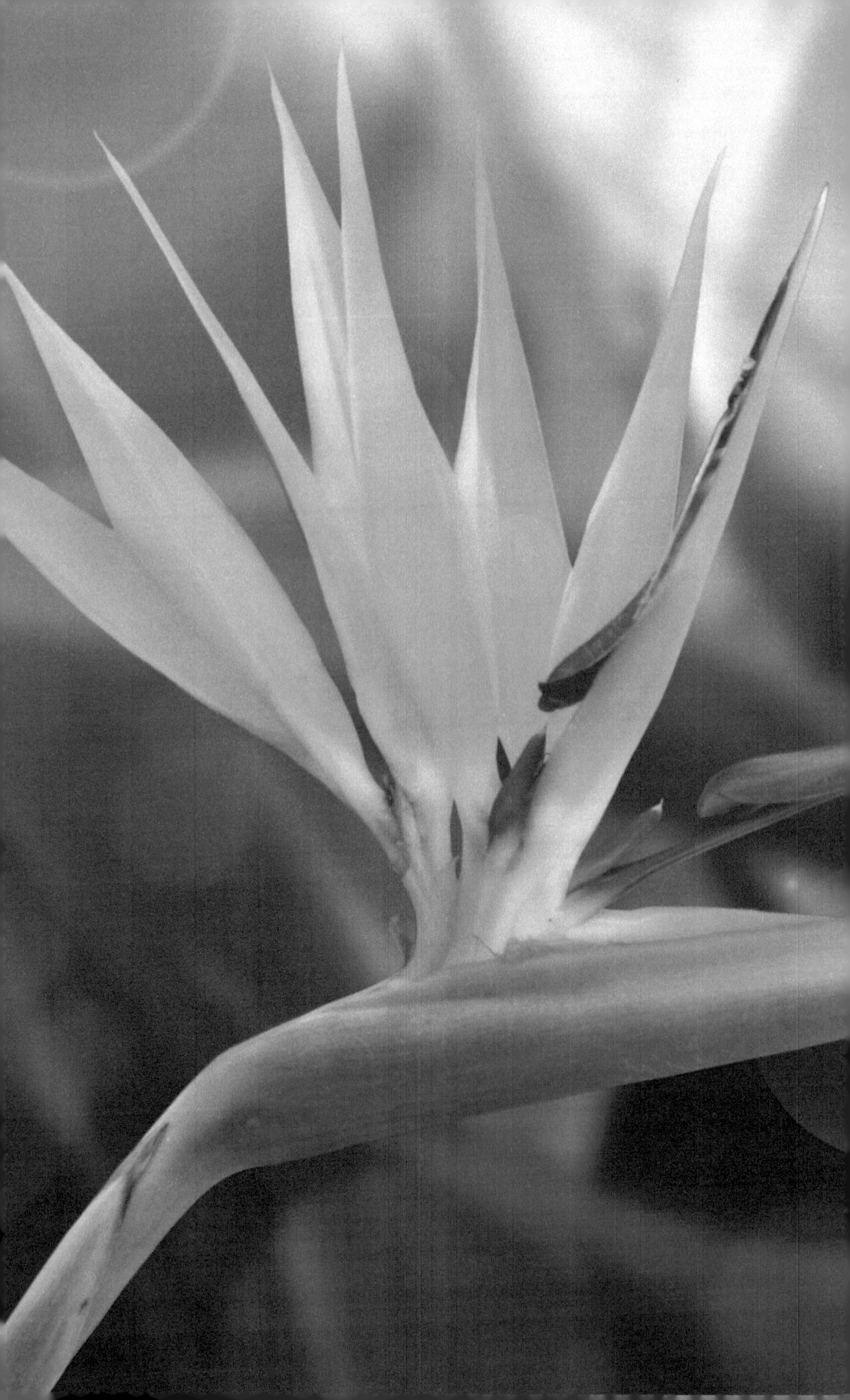

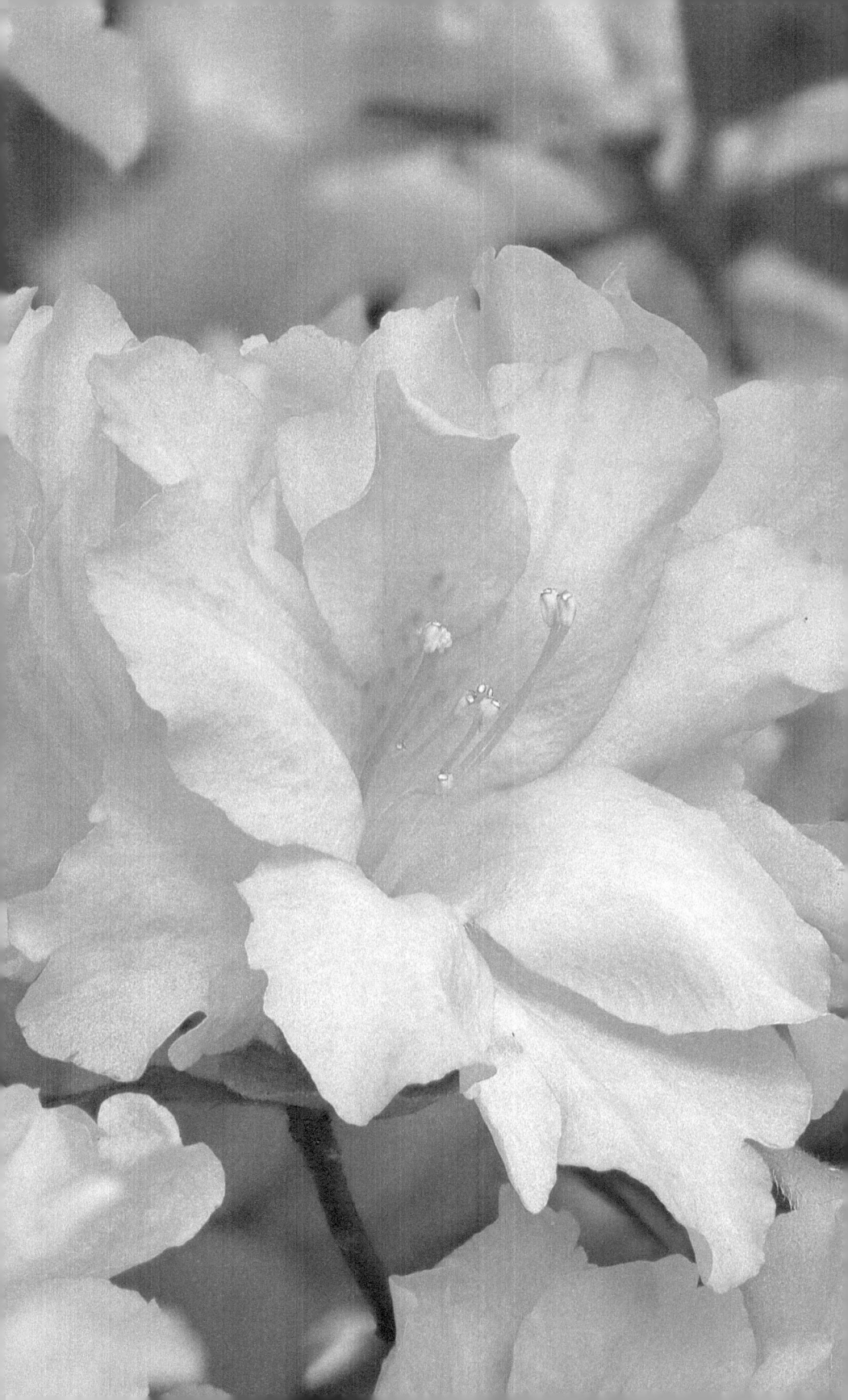

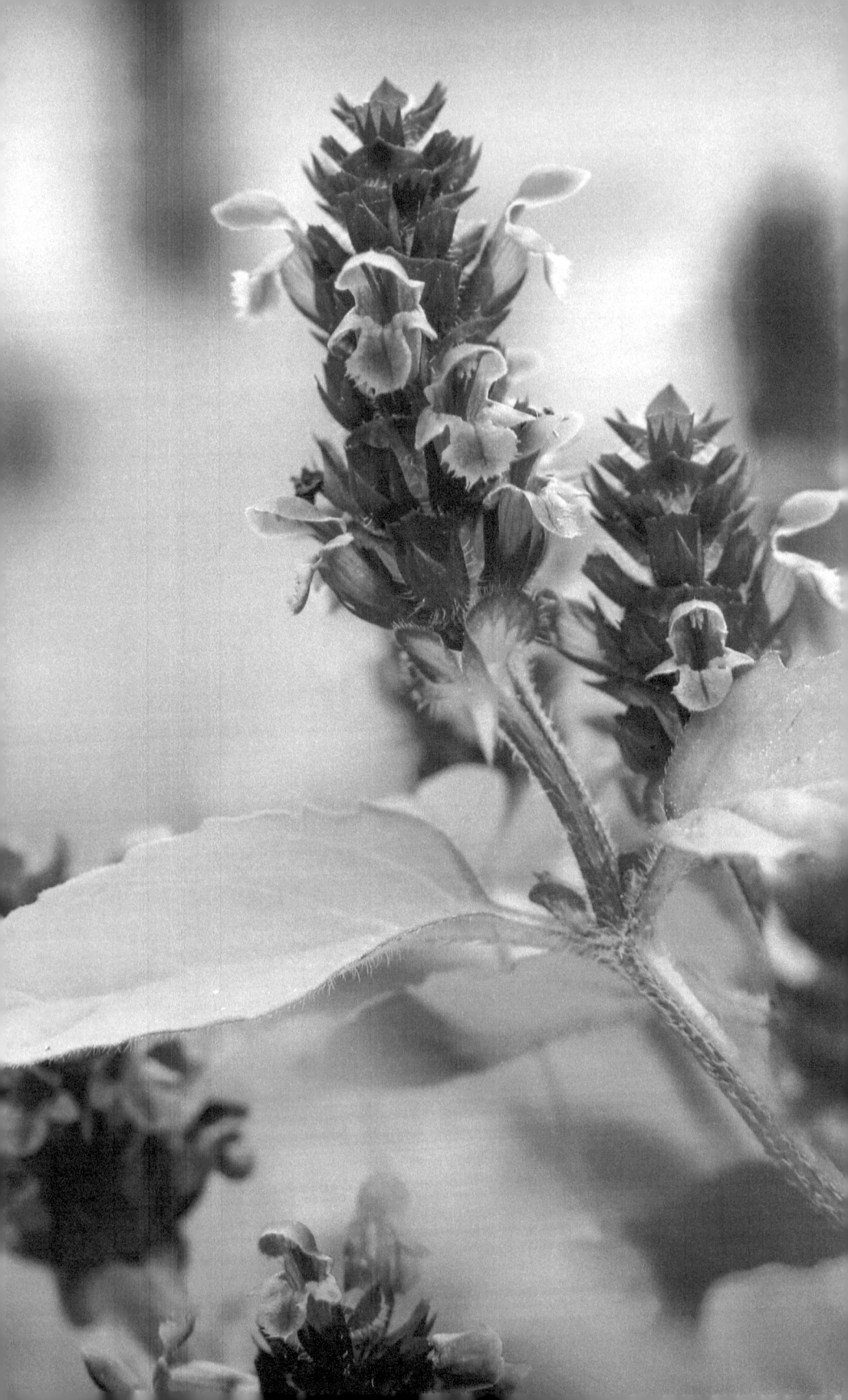

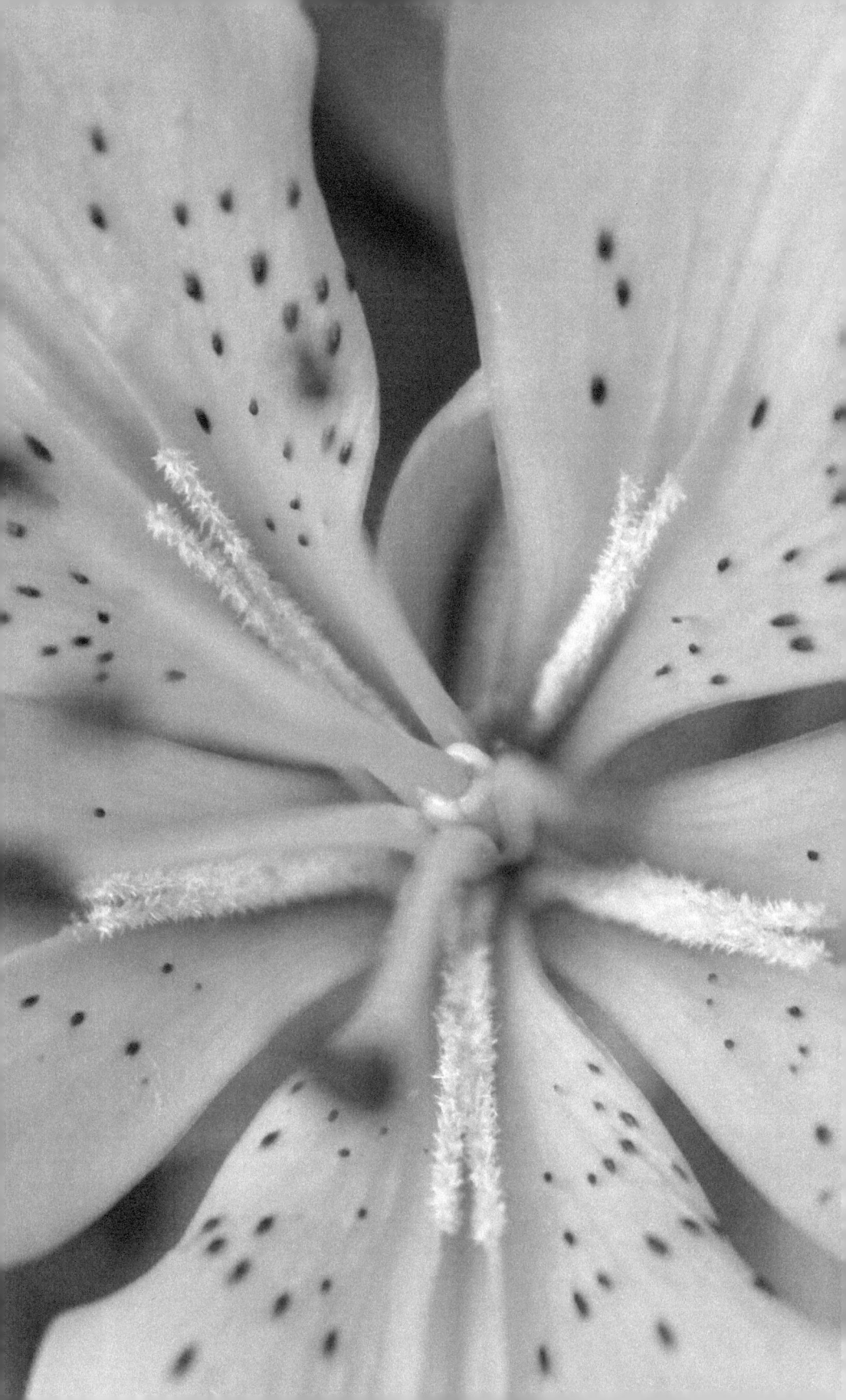

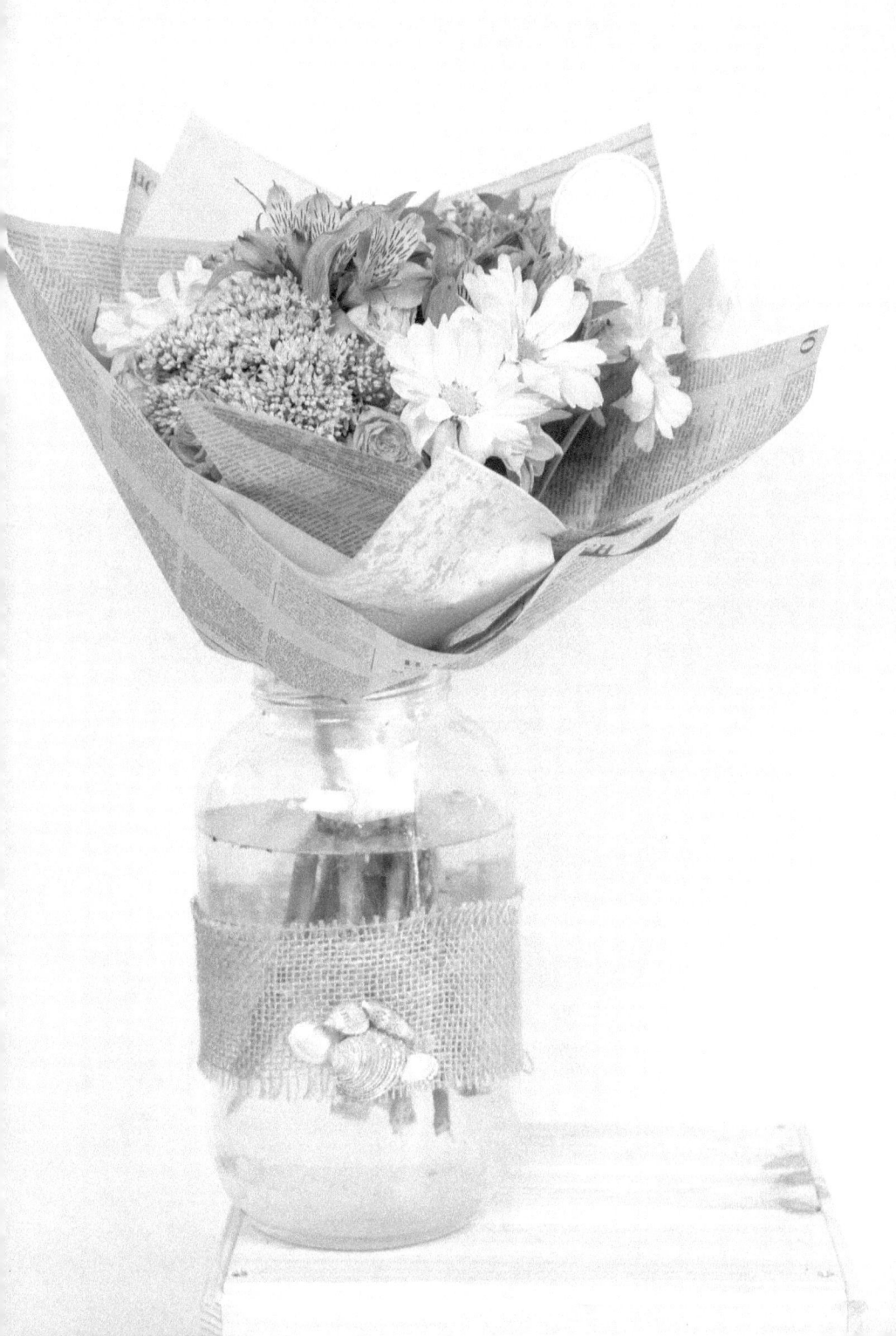

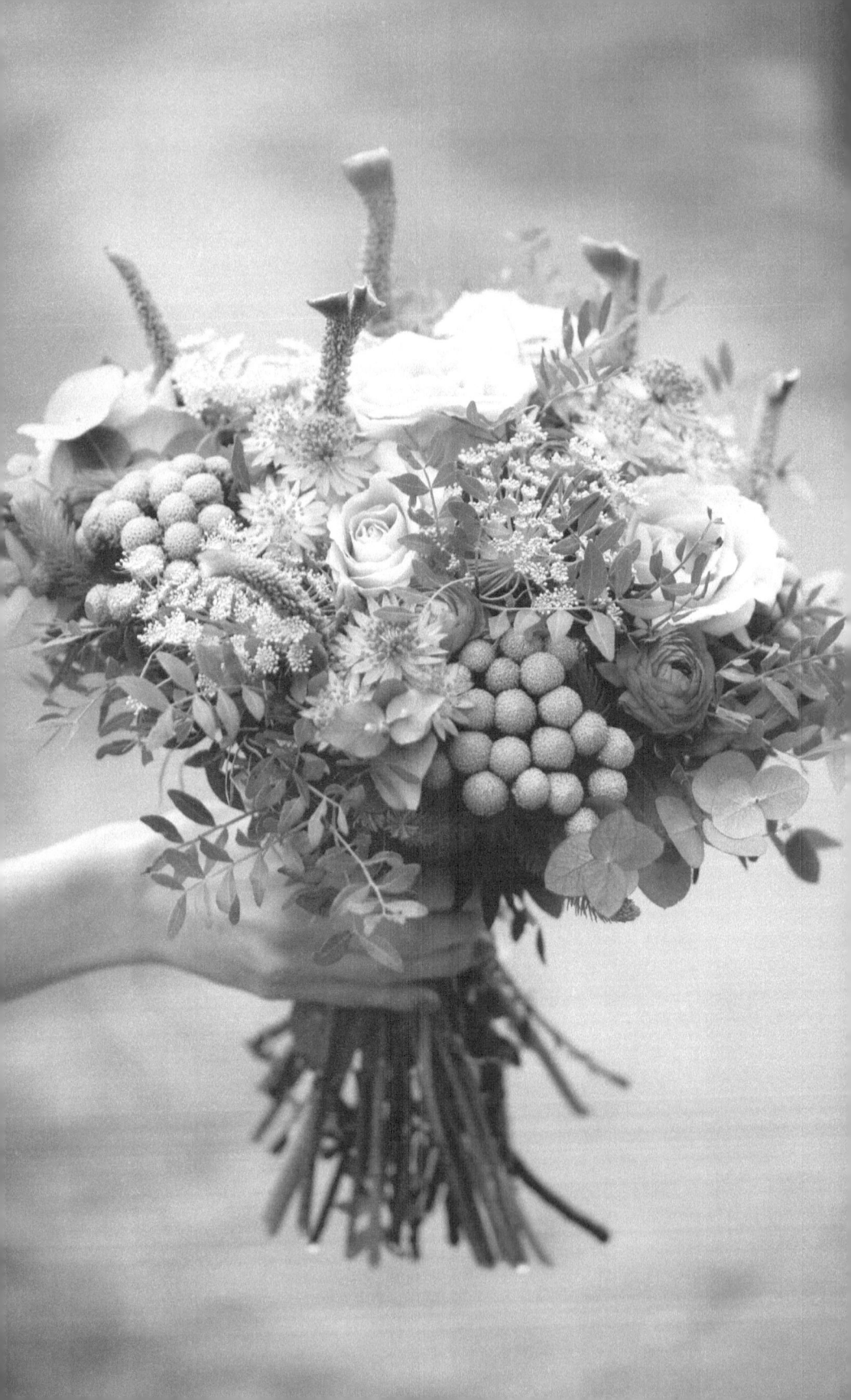

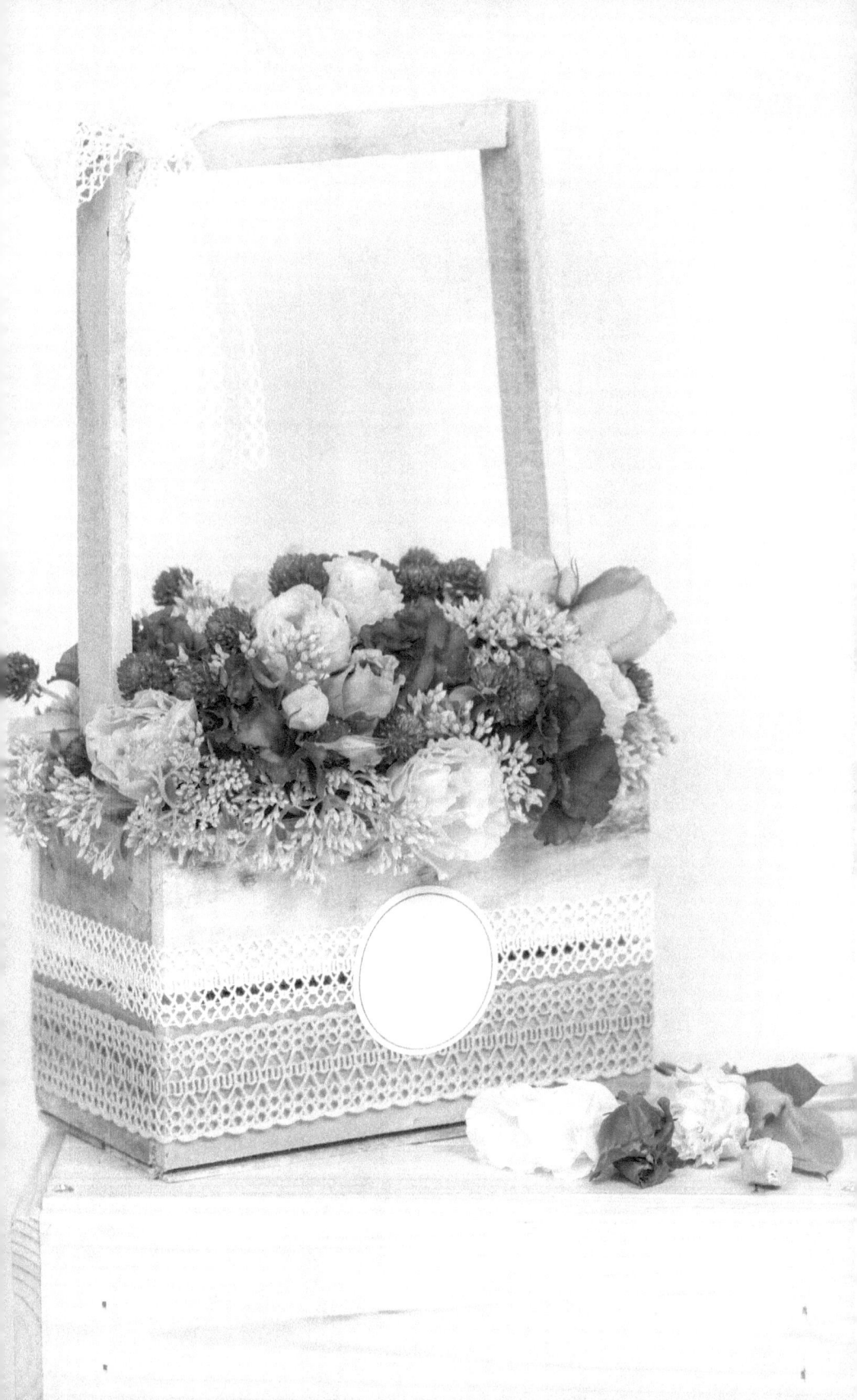

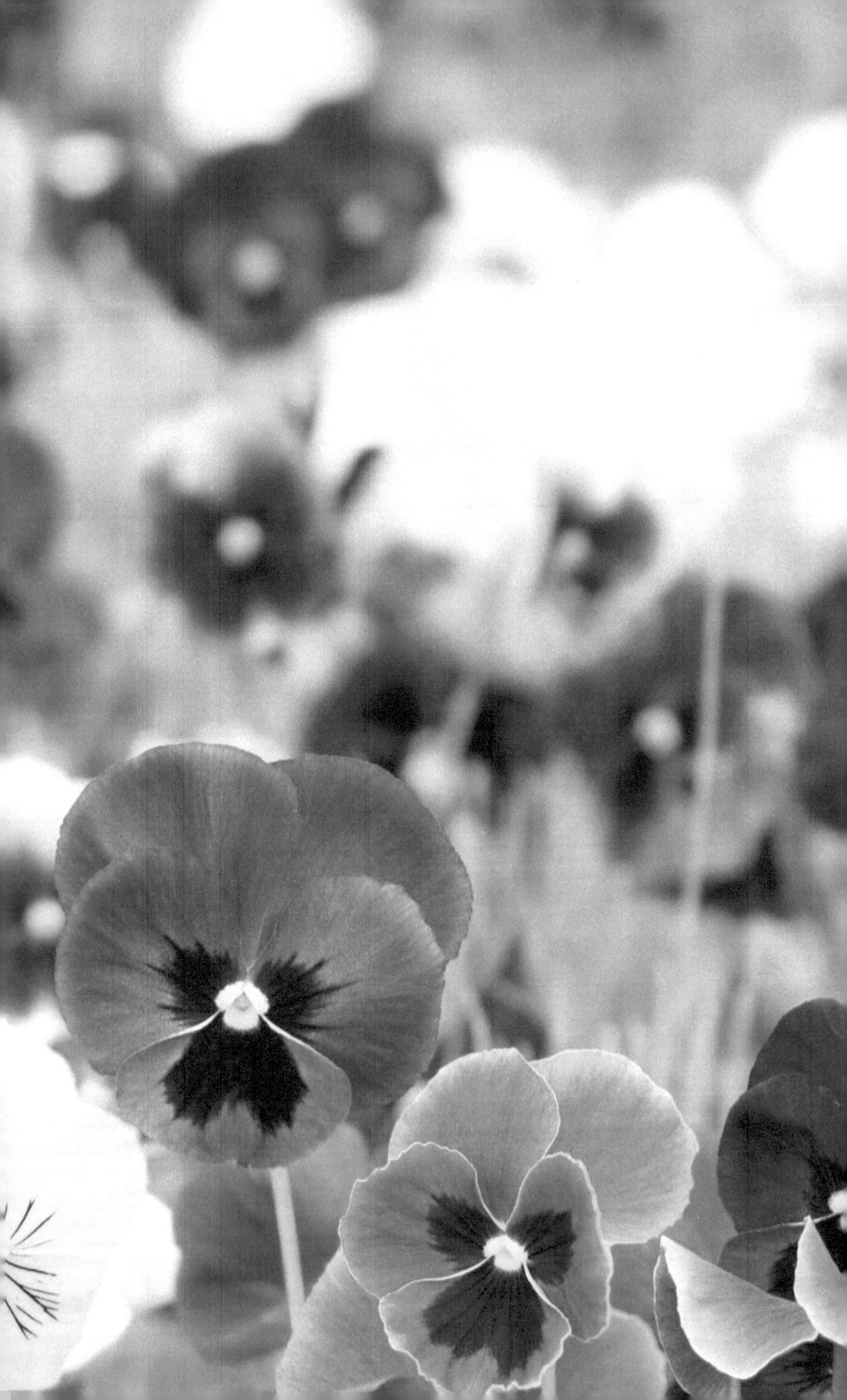

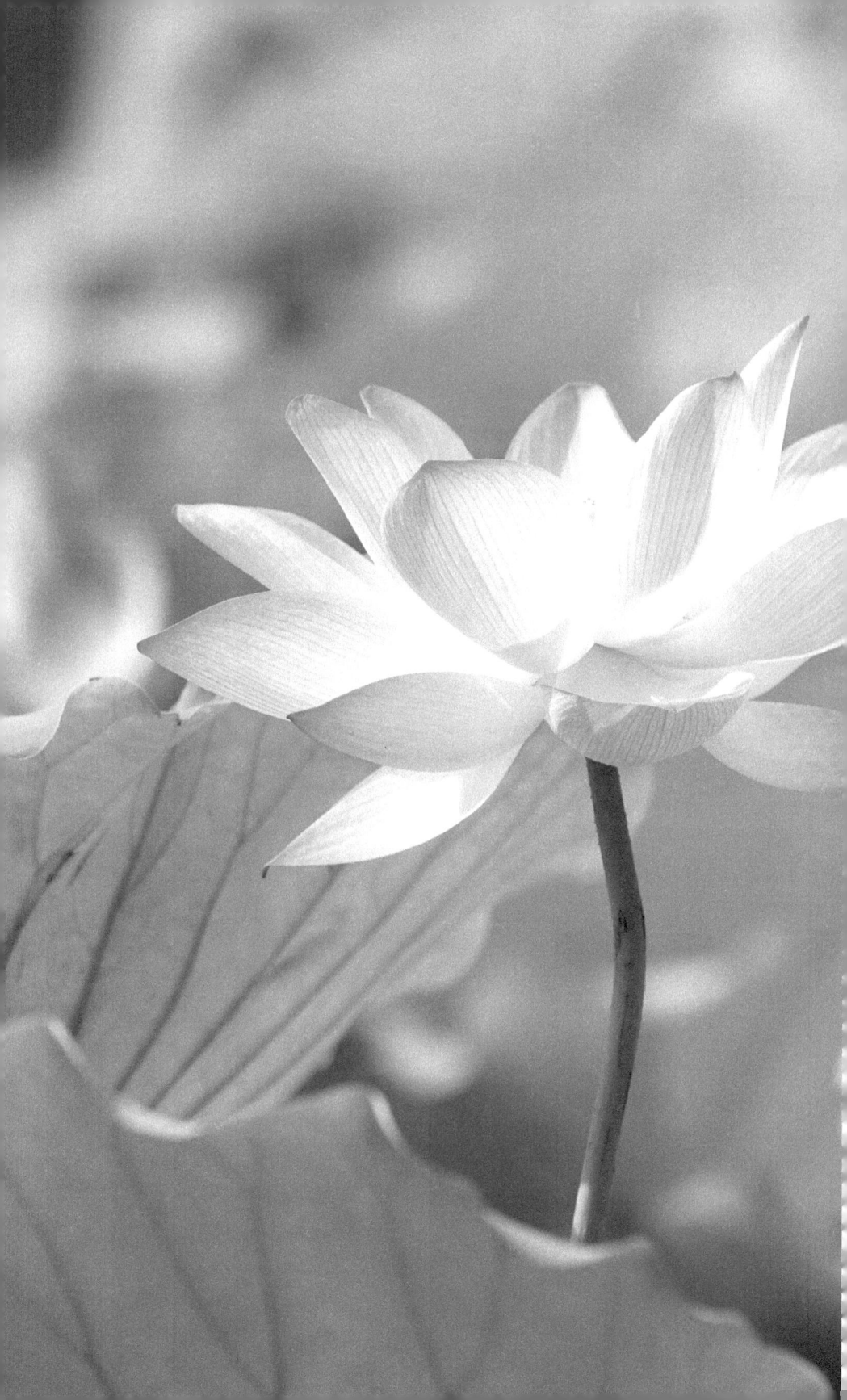

www.ingramcontent.com/pod-product-compliance
Lightning Source LLC
Chambersburg PA
CBHW021041180526
45163CB00005B/2231